Introducing Information System Management

Malcolm Peltu

Preface

Computer-based information systems are essential to the successful operation of most organisations. All managers must, therefore, have a realistic understanding of the benefits and limitations of the technologies involved; and Information System (IS) professionals must have a sound appreciation of the management and working environments they serve.

This book is a practical introductory guide to the key management and technical issues that contribute to the effective planning, development and operation of IS services. It will be of interest and value to anyone responsible for the management or provision of such systems. Students and researchers in business, management and information technology disciplines should also find the book helpful because of its comprehensive background to, and historical perspective on, such an important topic.

The book is written in plain language, with clear explanations of the main technical terms. It recommends the adoption of systematic strategies that promote effective partnerships between everyone involved in IS development and use. This approach is rooted in an awareness of actual organisational, social and personal behaviour, as well as the principles and potential of information technology. Chapter 3 is particularly significant in unifying the book's themes. It examines the general management techniques that provide the context within which information systems succeed or fail, and which explain why human and organisational factors are so crucial in determining the practical results to be achieved.

I would like to thank my colleagues and clients whose ideas and experiences have contributed so much to my own understanding.

Malcolm Peltu
Chiswick, January 1989

The National Computing Centre develops techniques, provides services, offers aids and supplies information to encourage the more effective use of Information Technology. The Centre co-operates with members and other organisations, including government bodies, to develop the use of computers and communications facilities. It provides advice, training and consultancy; evaluates software methods and tools; promotes standards and codes of practice; and publishes books.

Any interested company, organisation or individual can benefit from the work of the Centre — by exploring its products and services; or in particular by subscribing as a member. Throughout the country, members can participate in working parties, study groups and discussions; and can influence NCC policy.

For more information, contact the Centre at Oxford Road, Manchester M1 7ED (061-228 6333), or at one of the regional offices: London (01-353 4875), Bristol (0272-277 077), Birmingham (021-236 6283), Glasgow (041-204 1101) or Belfast (0232-665 997).

Do you want to write?

Could you write a book on an aspect of Information Technology? Have you already prepared a typescript? Why not send us your ideas, your 'embryo' text or your completed work? We are a prestigious publishing house with an international reputation. We have the funds and the expertise to support your writing ambitions in the most effective way.

Contact: Geoff Simons, Publications Division, The National Computing Centre Ltd, Oxford Road, Manchester M1 7ED.

Introduction

SUCCEEDING IN THE COMPUTER AGE

Computers are an essential ingredient in managing key aspects of most organisations. They help to cut administration costs and improve staff productivity. They keep managers in close touch with business performance. They assist in the design and manufacture of products. They improve the efficiency of interactions with clients, customers, suppliers and distribution outlets. They create opportunities for new services, products and business ventures.

The raw material worked on by computers to produce this wide range of benefits is *information:* orders, accounts, engineering data, medical records, personnel files, statistical analyses, information to be published, mathematical models, project plans, bank balances, and a multitude of other types of information — are all grist to the computing mill.

Computers can deal with information in the form of text, numbers, diagrams, voices, sounds, colours, handwriting, pictures and moving images. They can hold large amounts of information in ways that enable particular items to be easily found, updated, altered, compared, stored and manipulated.

Telecommunications links between computers and other devices can be used to transmit information between many locations.

The speed, efficiency and effectiveness with which they carry out these tasks have made computers the most widely used *information management* aid.

Information management is the set of policies and techniques used to collect, organise, analyse, process, communicate, and deliver information within and between organisations. This involves more than just a knowledge of how to use computers. Information management is also closely related to the general business and management practices employed. Organisational structures, for example, affect information flows within a company. The degree of centralisation or decentralisation of management decision-making also influences, and is influenced by, the ways in which information is gathered and distributed.

TURNING TECHNOLOGY INTO SYSTEMS

Information management often fails because it is treated as being primarily a technical function. It then tends to become shrouded in a fog of jargon, isolated from mainstream corporate decision-making processes.

Information management is also often incorrectly believed to be synonymous with two of its main constituents: *Information Technology* (*IT*) and *Information Systems* (*IS*). IT provides the tools to build information systems, which, in turn, implement information management policies.

IT emerged in the 1980s as a unified means of processing, analysing, storing and communicating almost any form of information. It represents the convergence of many modern innovations, including computers, microelectronics, telecommunications, and information recording and storage techniques.

The coherence of IT derives from two fundamental characteristics of computer-based systems:

> *Digital information.* Most forms of information can be represented in a code consisting only of the *bi*nary digi*ts (bits)* 0 and 1. Once information has been digitally encoded, it can be processed by computers and transmitted via telecommunications links.

> *Programmed control.* Computers process and manage information through *software,* detailed *programs* of instructions that control how the physical *hardware* operates. By changing software instructions, the same hardware can be applied to a huge variety of different user tasks. This 'soft centre' is the key to the computer's versatility.

Initial computer applications, starting in the 1960s and based on large centralised computers, were called *Data Processing* (*DP*). They were concerned primarily with administrative tasks, like accounting and payroll processing. The functions within organisations responsible for these became known as *Management Services* (*MS*) and *Management*

INTRODUCTION

Information Systems (*MIS*), as well as DP.

THE INFORMATION MANAGEMENT ROLE

As IT innovations helped computing move into an ever-widening range of applications, the need arose for greater corporate control of information systems. This led to the creation of the role of *Information Manager* (*IM*), also known as the *Chief Information Officer* (*CIO*).

The information manager's scope of responsibility extends beyond particular information systems. It encompasses the creation and development of policies, throughout the enterprise, which contribute positively to the evolution of successful corporate strategies and management controls. Information management must help to achieve corporate goals and influence what the goals are.

Figure I.1 summarises interactions between the main ingredients in information management: corporate strategy, information management policies, information systems, and IT.

Management direction devolves downwards from the enterprise's strategic goals and specific business tactics, which define the aims of information management policies. These policies are realised via IS developments using appropriate IT facilities. Of equal significance is the upward drive exerted by technological innovation on the opportunities opened for new corporate strategies, services, products and management initiatives.

KEEPING MANAGEMENT CONTROL

The interactions outlined in Figure I.1 are taking place within the context of the dynamic and complex environment created by modern economic, social, political and technological pressures. A balance must be maintained between all elements in the information management chain if these demands are to be met successfully.

Managers at all levels and in all areas of an enterprise must keep control over information systems. At the same time, management must be able to encourage and exploit the momentum from technological innovation which can be a powerful corporate success factor. In order to achieve this, a good understanding is needed of the:

— basic principles, jargon and potential of IT;

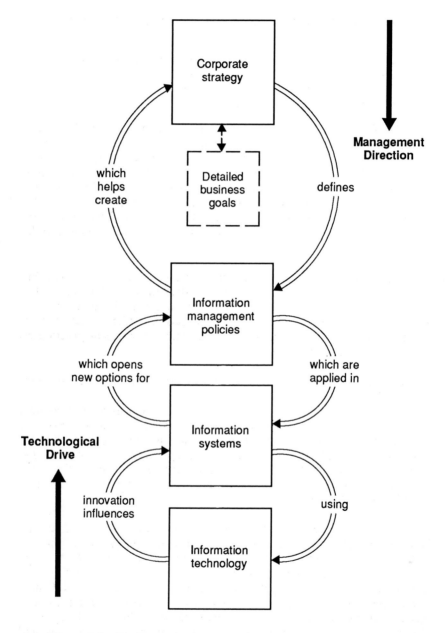

Figure I.1   Basic Information Management Interactions

— practical scope and limitations of using the technology in information systems;

— organisational behaviour and management approaches which shape the culture and practices of an enterprise and, therefore, determine the information management policies that will be most effective within a particular organisation.

The first part of this book (Chapters 1 to 3) describes the overall context in which information management operates and gives the essential background in each of these three areas. Chapter 1 focuses on IT, and Chapter 2 on information systems. Chapter 3 is particularly important because it describes the close relationship between information systems, the organisations in which they function and the people who manage, use and are affected by them. This corrects the misconceived view of information management as being almost exclusively concerned with technology.

Information management is increasingly dependent on IT, but successful exploitation of the technology depends on making computer-based information systems an integral part of how decisions are reached and work carried out within the organisation. Effective information management derives from applying the right management practices to relevant IS developments.

Subsequent chapters examine the issues raised in Part 1 in more depth.

Part 2 (Chapters 4 to 6) concentrates on the importance of developing systematic, realistic and flexible strategies and plans. Chapter 4 explores the corporate context in which information management policies operate. It explains the kind of strategy needed to manage the widespread impact of IS innovation. Chapter 5 defines the main ingredients of an information strategy. Chapter 6 outlines the contents of IS and IT strategies.

Part 3 (Chapters 7 to 12) systematically analyses the actions that should be taken to translate the broad strategies and plans discussed in Part 2 into successful live information systems. Chapter 7 sets the scene by describing key elements in the life cycle of an information system. Chapter 8 looks at how applications requirements should be investigated and specified, while Chapter 9 shows how appropriate solutions to these requirements should be evaluated and selected. Chapters 10 to 12 are concerned with vital practical aspects of developing, introducing and running information systems.

Contents

PART 1

Information Management in Perspective

1   Information Technology Background

STARTING BIG

Computers, originally solely mechanical devices, were conceived as mathematical 'number crunchers' by their nineteenth-century inventor Charles Babbage. In the Second World War, they received a military impetus when the first electronic computers were used for ballistic calculations and cryptographic code-breaking.

Many important computing innovations were made in the 1950s. These were confined mainly to research laboratories, except for a few pioneering attempts to apply computers to business needs. In 1954, for example, the British food company Lyons started a full commercial computing service based on its Lyon Electronic Office (LEO) computer. Until the 1960s, the most widespread forms of automated calculation devices used in business were tabulators, adding machines and comptometers, which had extremely limited computing capabilities.

The development of transistors and integrated circuits, to replace thermionic valves for basic electronic circuitry, helped computers to become more commercially viable in the early 1960s. Nevertheless, the first business computers were extremely large and had to be kept in machine rooms with controlled environments. They were known as *mainframes* because large structural frames were used to house components when each computer needed thousands of valves.

These mainframes could not be linked directly to any devices or other computers outside the machine room. Work, therefore, had to be brought to the computer, where it was handled by sequential *batch processing* methods. Results from this processing were produced largely in the form of printed reports, known as *printouts,* on special continuous stationery with relatively low-quality presentation.

Eventually, it became possible to link users directly *online* to mainframes via *terminals* connected by telecommunications lines. A typical terminal consists of a keyboard and screen, called a *Visual Display Unit* (*VDU*) or *Visual Display Terminal* (*VDT*). These are used typically to perform discrete transactions, such as making an airline reservation or finding an answer to a query. This is known as *Transaction Processing* (*TP*) applications.

Mainframes handle TP requirements by sharing resources between many different applications at the same time. The development of this *time-sharing* capability marked an important advance into the modern computer era.

COMPUTING MOVES DOWN THE LINE

During the 1960s, a breed of smaller, more robust and cheaper computers emerged, primarily in scientific and engineering-oriented applications. These *minicomputers* were widely used for tasks, like *process control* in chemical plants, which require instantaneous *real-time* analysis and responses. With TP, the user is usually content with *response times* of a few seconds to an online request, which would be unacceptable in real-time operations.

Minicomputers could run outside the special environments that were essential for mainframes. In the 1970s, they began to be introduced into commercial business environments in the form of small business systems. They carried out similar work to mainframes, but on a smaller scale. They could, however, be located much closer to users in ordinary office environments, with relatively small modifications to maintain necessary temperature and humidity conditions.

The growing use of small business systems, minicomputers, and terminals began to distribute business computing capabilities away from the central mainframe. As a result, a rapidly increasing amount of information had to be sent by telecommunications links between computers, and between computers and terminals. Telecommunications techniques, however, were traditionally based on a different information representation to the digital bits used by computers: until the 1970s, telecommunications transmission took place largely in *analogue* form. This deals in continuously varying quantities, as with sound-wave patterns produced by the human voice. The exchange switches used to route telecommunications connections were still largely electro-mechanical. The analogue nature of telecommunications constrained the geographical spread of computing capabilities. Analogue transmission limits the speed at which digitised information can be sent. In addition, information has to be translated between analogue and digital forms by special devices, called *modems* (*mod*ulators/*dem*odulators).

During the 1970s, however, computing and telecommunications technologies began to converge. Computers were used increasingly as telecommunications switches. Digital transmission became more common, boosted by the availability of communications media that can carry high volumes of data reliably, such as optical fibres, satellites and microwaves. For example, a pair of copper wires used traditionally in the telephone network can carry about 1.5 million bits per second (*bps*) — *its bandwidth*. A single optical fibre can carry over 1 billion bps and one cable can carry thousands of these hair-thin strands. This enabled extensive *networks* of computers and terminals to be built up, covering wide geographical areas. Central mainframes are important elements in the networks, but they have gradually lost their dominating role.

THE MICRO EXPLOSION

In January 1975, the American magazine *Popular Electronics* advertised a kit that could be used to build a small computer. It was the first hint of a revolution that would soon transform computing capabilities. The agent of that revolution was the *microchip*. Chips of silicon can be used in computers to process and store information. Each chip contains a number of transistors and other electronic components interconnected into *integrated circuits*. The number of components that can be included on a chip has a dramatic impact on the size, cost and power of computers.

The continuous increase in component density has been marked by naming the different levels of integration achieved, starting with Small Scale Integration (SSI), then moving through medium, large, very large, etc scales (known by their respective abbreviations: MSI, LSI and VLSI). Rapid progression through these stages led to chip costs falling by over 20% a year from the 1960s to 1980s. During this time, the complexity of chips increased at a similar rate. As a result, even more computing power has been packed into smaller spaces at lower prices. It was the incredible rate of these changes that triggered an explosive growth of computer-based systems and services in the 1980s.

The first complete computer processor on a chip was produced in 1971 by the American manufacturer Intel. A number of chips mounted on *boards* were needed to produce a complete computer. *Microcomputers,* able to fit onto a desk or table, constructed from such boards, became an increasingly popular hobby with young people after the initial *Popular Electronics* advertisement.

Two young American enthusiasts, Steven Jobs and Stephen Wozniak built their own microcomputer in a garage. They called it the Apple when it was launched in 1977 and it quickly began to bridge the gap between hobbyist and business computing.

BUSINESS COMPUTERS GET PERSONAL

Until the early 1980s, computers in business were seen primarily as a corporate resource to be applied to corporate applications. Even though networks, small business systems and minicomputers brought computers closer to the departments and people using them, only a few specialist users, like booking clerks, had a VDU on their own desk. Micro-computers were generally dismissed as being of interest only to amateurs and educationalists.

However, the micro-inspired drive towards cheap, compact, and powerful computers was irresistible. In 1981, the world's biggest computer manufacturer, IBM, introduced its Personal Computer. The name was chosen to reflect its break from traditional business computers by being oriented to the needs of individuals rather than departments or the organisation as a whole. The term *Personal Computer* (*PC*) is now generally used for all business microcomputers.

PCs initially had some similar limitations to their mainframe forebears in the early 1960s. They could be used for only one task at a time, as in batch processing, and could not be linked to other computers or devices. Of course, PCs have brought many advantages. They can, for example, be used on ordinary office desks. The user interacts directly with the computer via its screen and keyboard, which is similar in appearance to a VDU. Therefore, results are obtained immediately. In addition, PCs took full advantage of price/performance benefits generated by microchip innovation. A PC of the late 1980s gives hundreds of times greater performance than a 1960s mainframe or the 1970s small business systems — at less than 1% of the price. Even these comparisons underestimate progress, because a modern PC has capabilities like colour graphics, which were once beyond the scope of much larger and more expensive systems.

COMPUTING LANDSCAPES CHANGE

Advances in microelectronics have affected all computer-based systems, not just PCs. More cost-effective, powerful and versatile chips have increased the capabilities of mainframes and minicomputers. At one extreme, very fast *supercomputers* were developed primarily for scientific applications, like meteorology and university research programmes. At the smaller end, an imaginative variety of games computers, advanced calculators, electronic diaries and other products became available in the consumer market.

Between these two extremes, distinctions between different computer categories have been blurred. Mainframes became smaller. The capabilities of some minicomputers overtook those of some mainframes. A category of *superminicomputers* grew to cover 'minicomputers' that provide the performance previously associated only with 'mainframes'. Some PCs are now able to handle many tasks for one user at a time (known as *multi-tasking*) and for many users to be connected to a system simultaneously (the *multi-user* capability). Communications enhancements to PCs have enabled them to be linked to each other and to other systems. Multi-user PCs and PC networks can now often provide a viable alternative to minicomputers, small business systems and smaller mainframes.

Chips also brought *intelligence* to terminals, like VDUs. Initially, terminals were called *dumb* because they had no capabilities of their own for processing information and minimal, if any, storage facilities. They relied on the computers to which they were connected to perform the required functions. The ability to introduce chips into terminals gave the devices the 'intelligence' to handle many computing tasks independently. Terminals became known as *workstations* to reflect this change. VDUs evolved to provide additional capabilities that need more in-built computing capabilities than the simple display of a single frame of text filling the whole screen. Displays can now have many frames on a screen at the same time, each of which can be used for a different purpose. New ways of interacting with a VDU, in addition to a keyboard, have been incorporated into modern workstations — such as touch-sensitive screens and pointers. *Graphics workstations* can display complex images with great clarity. Indeed, some workstations incorporate the computing power of a PC or minicomputer.

The distinction between different categories of computer has, therefore, become blurred. It is irrelevant whether a particular system is called a 'mainframe' or 'supermini'; a 'minicomputer' or 'low-end mainframe'; a 'workstation' or 'personal computer' or 'intelligent terminal'. What matters are the facilities they provide; how they meet real user needs; and how much they cost in practical use.

THE VITAL SOFT CENTRE

There are two main types of software:

> *Systems software* controls, co-ordinates, and manages hardware and communications resources. A basic systems software function is the *operating system,* which co-ordinates all basic resources, such as multi-tasking and multi-user control. The sharing of computerised information between many users and applications is handled by systems software called a *Database Management System* (*DBMS*). Programs that handle networking and communications are also important systems software.

> *Applications software* deals directly with users' activities. The range of applications software that can run on particular hardware is usually determined primarily by the operating system and other systems software.

Software programs define, in precise detail, the complex procedures and operations that a computer must perform to meet user needs. As user requirements evolve, software must evolve with them. These instructions are written in special *programming languages* and *program code.*

Software is extremely complex to develop, modify and enhance. Some software systems consist of hundreds of thousands, or even millions, of instructions. When errors, known as *bugs,* occur in programs, the *debugging* process of finding and correcting them can be time-consuming and difficult. In fact, programmers often spend most of their time debugging and maintaining existing software, rather than writing new program code.

Since software first emerged as a major force in the 1950s, substantial progress has been made in understanding the software development process and in providing systematic methodologies to support it. These *software engineering* advances have been boosted in the 1980s with the help of *Computer Aided Software Engineering* (*CASE*) tools. However, the pace of software engineering improvements has failed to keep up with the growth in demand inspired by hardware price/performance enhancements. The availability of cheaper and smaller hardware rapidly expands the volume of software systems that are needed. More powerful hardware, particularly in linked networks, adds significantly to software complexities.

At the same time, the productivity of highly paid computing professionals has risen much more slowly than equivalent hardware gains. The result has been steadily rising software costs compared to the dramatic decline in the relative value of the hardware elements of systems. PC software is available at considerably lower unit prices than mainframe and minicomputer software because of the substantially higher sales volumes that can be achieved, rather than through lower development costs. Efficient and effective control over software is one of the major challenges in managing information systems. The issues involved are examined in more detail in Chapter 10.

MAKING COMPUTERS MORE FRIENDLY

General

Originally, computers were designed largely *by* computer experts *for* computer experts. Hardly any attention was given to what non-technical users wanted until computers started to be used directly in offices by managers, professionals, secretaries, typists, clerks and others who have little computing knowhow. The computer experts then realised that their systems would not be utilised to their full potential unless they became more friendly to all users.

This led to increasing research into making computer systems easier to understand and use without a great deal of prior training. These *ergonomic* and *human factors engineering* studies focused on what has become known variously as *Human-Computer Interaction* (*HCI*) and *Man-Machine Interface* or *Man-Machine Interaction* (*MMI*). They are concerned both with hardware and software factors. On the hardware side, there are aspects like the quality of screen displays (character legibility, glare, etc) and the layout of the keyboard. Software controls the nature of the dialogue between the user and the system, such as the commands needed to initiate actions and the presentation of information on a screen.

The WIMP Interface

In the mid-1970s, an office automation project at Xerox Corporation's Palo Alto Research Centre (PARC) in California developed an approach to screen-based workstations which brought interactions closer to the natural way people behave in offices. The project saw the screen as a 'desk top' on which a number of documents may lie and from which users can carry out several tasks at a time. Facilities were also provided to enable users to interact with information on the screen in ways other than via a keyboard and purely textual messages on a single-frame screen.

The interface developed at PARC is sometimes called *WIMP* after:

Windows, which enable a workstation screen to be subdivided into a number of smaller areas. Each of these inset windows acts as if it were an independent screen, so that the user can see different documents or results from different applications on one screen simultaneously.

Icons, which represent various functions available within the system by the use of small diagrams which illustrate the activity, such as a filing cabinet for files.

Menus, which present information on a screen in the form of a number of options, from which the user has to select one to initiate an action or to move onto another menu. *Pop-up* menus appear as windows on the screen at appropriate points in an interaction.

Pointers, which let the user move a marker on the screen to carry out operations, such as pointing to an icon or identifying where in a document information should be moved to. The most widely used pointer is the *mouse,* so named because that is what it looks like. It is a small device that fits in the palm of the hand. As it is moved around on the desk, the marker on the screen moves in the same direction. Appropriate actions are initiated by keys on the mouse.

The WIMP approach was popularised in the 1980s on the Apple Macintosh computer and it has now become the basis for many other systems. Further discussion on human factors requirements is provided in Chapter 9.

CONVERGENCE INTO INFORMATION TECHNOLOGY

The technological discussion so far has indicated how microelectronics, computing and telecommunications developments have overlapped. This is part of the wider convergence into IT which encompasses many developments with long traditions of their own, including:

Computing. Computers are at the heart of IT, enabling systems to be adapted to a great variety of applications. Most IT now operates in the digital code used by computers.

Microelectronics. Microchips have enormously expanded the scope of IT applications because they dramatically improved computing performance, reliability, and robustness, while cutting the size and cost of computers at a rapid rate.

Telecommunications. Building on existing telephone networks, advanced national and international *Wide Area Networks* (*WANs*) have been created to handle the interlinking of computers, workstations and other devices over varied geographical areas; *Local Area Networks* (*LANs*) cover smaller expanses, such as an office or building. Telecommunications performance, particularly using digital transmission, has been greatly enhanced through advances like computerised exchanges, satellites, and optical fibres. The enforcement of international and industry-wide standards is particularly vital in networking and telecommunications, because users often want to interconnect systems from many suppliers.

Advanced telephony. Flexible and sophisticated telephone services have been made available by the use of computerised telephone exchanges and the introduction of microchips into telephone handsets and answering machines. Facilities like automatic call rerouteing and telephones with memories are now common. Car phones have also become feasible through *cellular radio* networks. Areas within the network are divided into cells, each with its own radio frequency. As a car travels between cells, computers change frequency automatically. The cellular network links directly to the public telephone system.

Mail. Documents and messages can now be sent through *electronic mail* techniques, for example by networks linking word processors, personal computers, workstations and high speed, high quality printers. *Facsimile* (*fax*) transmission of documents has been significantly enhanced through advances in fax devices and telecommunications capabilities. Traditional telex services can be linked to computer-based networks via the *teletex* facility.

Information storage. Digital information for computer use can be stored on the same, or similar, media to those used for music and home entertainment, including audio tapes and discs, video tape and compact discs. (In computing, the American spelling *disk* is usually used.) The storage media used directly by computers include flexible (*floppy*) disks in smaller systems, like word processors and personal computers; *hard disks* for larger volumes of information; and *optical disks,* similar to compact discs, for holding images, such as 'pictures' of document pages.

Filing, libraries, and access to information. Computer databases store, manage, share and distribute large volumes of information which can be accessed quickly through online interaction if needed. This has created opportunities for sharing information between many people, locations, stores, branches, departments, warehouses, depots, suppliers, organisations and so on.

Typing. The first automatic typewriter was produced in the 1920s. It was only in the 1970s, however, that computer-based *word processing* substantially improved the ease and efficiency with which documents may be typed and printed. Word processors enable text to be entered directly from a keyboard into computer memory, using a screen to display the text. Text can also be stored in the word processor for subsequent automatic reproduction; for example, in mail-shot letters or standard clauses in legal contracts.

Publishing. Computerised typesetting and composition systems have significantly improved the speed and efficiency of producing newspapers, magazines and books. Combined with the capabilities of personal computers, these facilities have been brought within the scope of ordinary offices with *Desk Top Publishing* (*DTP*) systems. They can use advanced printing technques, like *laser printers,* that silently produce reasonably high quality and versatile output at reasonably low cost.

Manufacturing design and production. Computers can help in all stages of the design and manufacture of products. For example, *Computer Aided Design* (*CAD*) techniques use graphics workstations to develop product designs and to automate the drafting of detailed drawings. *Computer Aided Manufacture* (*CAM*) covers the planning, control and production phases of manufacturing. On the production line, computers and microchips have produced sophisticated *Computer Numerical Control* (*CNC*) machine tools and robots to carry out routine production line work. These systems can be combined into a *Computer Integrated Manufacturing* (*CIM*) environment.

Retail technology. Computer-based *Electronic Point of Sale* (*EPOS*) terminals have replaced many cash registers. As well as calculating customer charges, they can gather information automatically on stock movements. When products have been labelled with bar codes, the EPOS terminal can read the codes directly to find out the product type and price.

Television. The transmission of television pictures is increasingly being carried out through new telecommunications media, like satellites and optical fibre cables. Television signals are also being used to transmit digital information, such as the *teletext* news services that enables users to select pages of information to be displayed on their television screens. Television sets can also be linked via telephone lines to *videotex* services, such as British Telecom's *viewdata*, which enables users to interact with its database, eg by ordering a product, as well as looking up information. Services like videotex and teletext are obtained by incorporating chips into TV sets and using keypads and keyboards to interact with the service, so the TV set becomes equivalent to a VDU.

Training and education. Computers can be used to provide programmed learning courses that can be followed at the pace and in the directions chosen by the student when interacting with the instructional software. Such *Computer Aided Instruction* (*CAI*) programs can be combined with video tape or optical disks to provide *interactive video* systems which include moving or still images in the course. These systems are also known as *Computer Aided Learning* (*CAL*) and *Computer Aided Training* (*CAT*).

TOWARDS INTEGRATED SOLUTIONS

Information Technology is more than just an umbrella term for a variety of distinct devices, systems, techniques and methodologies which handle information in some way. It is a unique force, synthesising its constituent elements into an integrated approach to the management of information.

As discussed earlier, distinctions between different types of computer-based services are being blurred. The same hardware can be used for a range of applications, depending on the software used. A varied mix of different types of devices and systems can be interlinked in networks. Once an integrated network has been established, it can be extended over time to encompass new applications, new users and new locations. For example, an office system could include many word processors, PCs and other workstations that can operate independently to satisfy the needs of an individual or a small group. These could be connected in a network which enables electronic mail to be sent between devices. The 'mail' could include a mix of information types, such as the merging of text and voices into *voice memos*. When a person is preparing a document on a word processor, it may be possible to record a voice message at a particular point. When the recipient sees the voice/memo icon on the screen, he or she plays it back, as you would with a tape recorder.

The office network with personal workstations could also be connected to a *departmental computer*, typically a supermini or small mainframe, which is used for sharing database information needed by many people in a particular organisational unit. There could also be links to central corporate mainframes and other departmental computers.

Once the internal network has been established, direct links can be made to other organisations, such as suppliers, or directly to customers and clients. In retail organisations, a network could include EPOS terminals and in-store minicomputers; links between stores and warehouses and between warehouses and suppliers; CAD terminals for store designs; desk top publishing for marketing and public relations activities; and the office systems, departmental and corporate computers already discussed. Additional stores, warehouses, offices and suppliers could be added when needed. New services, such as home ordering via videotex terminals, could also be incorporated. IT is, therefore, an important tool in providing efficient, integrated information management solutions.

ARCHITECTURES FOR THE FUTURE

Basic computer and information systems *architectures* have evolved to cope with the transition from batch to distributed applications. There are two main architectural considerations: the basic structure of computers and the way communications networks are handled.

Von Neumann Architectures

Traditionally, computers were based on the *von Neumann architecture*, named after American computer pioneer John von Neumann. This had a single *Central Processing Unit* (*CPU*) with associated main memory. This was adequate for batch processing, but it became an increasing bottleneck for multi-user online and networked systems. The CPU, for example, had to handle all communications interruptions, as well as processing the actual workload.

The first three 'generations' of computers were marked by hardware progress within the von Neumann framework. *First generation* computers used thermionic valves. The *second generation* introduced transistors and the *third generation* had integrated circuits.

User-oriented Architectures

The availability of low cost microchips helped computer designers to move computer processing capabilities to different parts of a system. For instance, special processors have been developed to control disks and *Input/Output* (*I/O*) devices, such as terminals and printers. Interest was also shown in developing architectures with the flexibility and performance needed for database and communications applications. Such user-oriented approaches to architectures, involving a greater distribution of processing and memory facilities within a system, became known as the *fourth generation*, which has never had as clear-cut a definition as the first three.

The *fifth generation*, however, was clearly defined in 1979 by a Japanese government report. It seeks to incorporate a variety of advanced developments, including:

— *Artificial Intelligence* (*AI*) techniques, such as *expert systems*, to help enable computers to reason and 'think' in similar ways to people, in contrast to the traditional machine-like logic into which all applications had to be translated with previous generations;

— user interfaces that support the way people naturally perform a task;

— continuing deployment of advances in the speed, cost, reliability and compactness of hardware to improve overall systems performance.

Network Architectures

Network architectures are concerned with the relationships between elements in a network, such as the location of *nodes* through which communications are co-ordinated, the routes that connect various devices and systems and the technical standards used for communications. The lack of compatibility between communications architectures from different suppliers meant that users became 'locked in' to the range of equipment and facilities offered for a particular architecture. The importance of having greater flexibility of communications in creating integrated information systems has led to international efforts to provide agreed industry-wide standards, discussed in the next section.

HOW STANDARDS PROMOTE FLEXIBILITY

Maximum benefits will be gained from IT convergence and integration only if users have complete flexibility in choosing the most appropriate solution for a particular need, without having to spend significant effort and money in making the new system compatible with existing ones.

In such an *open system*, the following key capabilities should be provided:

Communications connectivity. It should be possible to interlink all types of devices and systems, along any routes, via simple connecting mechanisms.

Device compatibility. Devices, like disks and printers, should be easily exchangeable between systems.

Software portability. Programs should be capable of being moved between different systems quickly and efficiently with minimal, if any, alteration to code.

Information storage consistency. It should be possible to move stored computerised information between any hardware and software, without having to worry about different physical characteristics of storage media or the encoded formats in which information is recorded.

In the past, however, incompatibilities between systems were the norm due to a lack of widely agreed standards in the industry. It has also often been in suppliers' self-interest to make their systems incompatible with those of other manufacturers because the cost of conversion would discourage users from moving to systems from other vendors.

Basic program instructions and information storage codes used by different computers vary considerably. The same programming language can have many 'dialects' which prevent programs from being portable, even when systems support the same language. Most significantly, operating systems are usually specific to a particular hardware range. This limits the portability of applications software written to be compatible with specific operating system interfaces.

Over time, a number of standards have been developed to overcome incompatiblity problems. Some standards have resulted from the *de facto* dominance of a product in a particular market sector. Others have come about because national and international standards bodies, large corporations and government organisations have taken the initiative to promote compatibility. IT convergence has also forced most suppliers to realise that their long-term sales growth depends on agreeing standards that encourage simpler and more efficient development of integrated systems.

Creating Open Systems

One of the most significant standardisation efforts in the 1980s is the *International Standards Organisation* (*ISO*) proposals on *Open System Interconnection* (*OSI*) communications. The term 'open system' derives from this work. OSI defines a series of rules and conventions, known as *protocols*, which govern how computer communications take place. Seven OSI protocol layers have been defined, ranging from detailed electrical and other physical connections at Level 1 to the overall user application at Level 7.

The seven-layer OSI *stack* can be adapted to many applications. For example, the *Manufacturing Automation Protocol* (*MAP*) has been developed for production activities and the *Technical and Office Protocol* (*TOP*) for office automation. Large users of computers have been prominent in OSI activities. MAP standardisation efforts, for example, have been spearheaded by General Motors, the automobile manufacturer, and TOP by the aerospace giant, Boeing. In addition, most leading IT suppliers have committed themselves to OSI's general aims.

OSI will not, however, be an overnight panacea to solve all problems caused by the lack of IT standardisation. Its detailed protocols are most well defined at the lower levels, closer to physical transmission than user applications. OSI is also concerned only with communications needs. Other key issues for standardisation, like operating systems and general software portability, are outside its scope, but there are a number of internationally co-ordinated standards activities in other areas, eg programming languages, like COBOL, Ada and FORTRAN, and the Unix operating system.

However, even if agreement is reached on all key standards and portability requirements, users will still face problems with older, pre-standardisation systems. Organisations will not want to replace a system that is currently providing a reasonably successful service just because it fails to meet the latest standards. Bridging and conversion aids for older systems will, therefore, be a continuing need.

Nevertheless, standardisation makes a substantial contribution to improving the benefits that users can gain from IT. Standards cut costs by reducing, or eliminating, the effort needed to integrate new systems and applications into an existing service. Standards also increase user choice, enabling the most cost-effective solution to be chosen for each application. Such flexibility significantly enhances the scope, efficiency and effectiveness of integrated IT solutions. Encouraging a commitment to widely agreed standards should, therefore, be a top management priority in any organisation making substantial use of computer-based systems.

SUMMARY: CONVERGENCE, DIVERGENCE AND INTEGRATION

It is worth summarising the main themes in this chapter:

Convergence. A variety of technological developments have converged to form IT. Digital information representation and software-based computer control are the key principles that bind the varied constituents of IT into a unified force.

Divergence. IT is being applied to a diverse range of activities covering corporate, departmental and individual requirements in many locations. The main technological engine stimulating ventures into new applications territory is microelectronics. The microchip has dramatically cut the cost and size of computers while increasing their power and range of capabilities. This has enabled computer-based systems to become a cost-effective solution in activities where their use would have been impractical, or even inconceivable, a few years ago.

Integration. The full flowering of applications nourished by IT's innovatory roots will come by effectively integrating different types of systems, software, communications links and devices. The development, agreement and implementation of standards among IT suppliers and users is a vital contributor to efficient and reliable methods of integration.

2 How Business Information Systems Evolved

SYSTEMS WITHOUT COMPUTERS

An information system is concerned with procedures such as:

— how and where information is gathered;

— how information flows through the organisation and groups within it;

— who should receive particular documents or types of information;

— what calculations and procedures are used to process information;

— how people carry out information-handling tasks most effectively;

— how and where documents and information are stored;

— patterns of communication between individuals and groups within the organisation and with outsiders, such as clients, suppliers and agents;

— who should be told if particular events occur — and how much they should be told;

— how decisions are made and what information is needed to make them;

— frequency of information processing events, such as enquiries, sales orders, production of letters, payment of invoices, updates to production plans, etc;

— what documents and forms are used for particular tasks;

— how information errors are dealt with, and minimised;

— what regular reports are needed: how frequently, who should get them, and what they should contain;

— what information various managers need to monitor work performance, and how the information is gathered and disseminated.

All these activities may *or may not* use IT. In pre-computing days, they were governed largely by procedures and rules defined by organisational charts, procedure manuals, job descriptions, and practices derived from experience and tradition. Since the 1960s, however, the computing content of information systems has grown significantly.

COMPUTERS MOVE IN

The characteristics of batch processing mainframe computers had a strong influence on how computers were introduced into organisations. The high costs of mainframes, for what were still unproven benefits, naturally brought them under close scrutiny from finance directors. Their 'mathematical' connotations also made accounting seem to be one of the most obvious applications. It was clear, however, that the innovative technical complexities of computers placed them outside the knowhow of existing financial and accounting personnel. This led to the creation of specialist DP departments reporting to the finance director.

The size of mainframes and their need for machine rooms with special environmental controls frequently led to the physical isolation of the DP department from the rest of the organisation. This separation was often emphasised by the unique jargon, ways of working, appearance, salary expectations and career ambitions (usually within the computing profession, not the organisation) of DP specialists.

A Slow Takeoff with Routine Administration

The availability of only batch processing capabilities meant DP departments initially focused primarily on predictable, routine tasks, such as ledger accounting, invoicing, payroll processing and stock (also called *inventory*) control. Even today, the formats of information in these applications are generally so stable that data structures can be predefined. A typical DP *file* structure may consist of a number of *records* (eg one per employee in a personnel file), divided into many *fields*, such as name, staff number, department, etc.

Information in records was kept as short as possible in order to minimise the need for expensive hardware storage facilities. There could be a large number of records and many files, so abbreviations and numeric codes were used in individual fields to keep down the overall size of files. This kind of structured, abbreviated information is still in use and is often referred to as *data* to distinguish it from text, graphics, voice and other types of information.

Despite its limited scope of application, data processing became commonplace in most medium to large organisations by the 1970s. This was partly due to the undeniable benefits achieved by applications which significantly improved administrative efficiency. There was also considerable momentum built up by a general feeling that computers were a key technology of the future and a fear that competitors could gain considerable advantages by using them more quickly and effectively.

SHARING INFORMATION EFFICIENTLY

Once the considerable investment in computing became an entrenched part of an organisation's operations, management obviously wanted to exploit its potential as much as possible. This created a steady growth in computer applications and in the amount and variety of information held on computer databases. Much of this data was common to many applications.

The traditional *file management* techniques developed for batch data processing applications are an inefficient way of managing a database that has to share its information. Such files evolved in an *ad hoc* way; new ones were created for specific applications, although there was considerable overlap with data in existing files. This meant much data was duplicated, such as having part-number fields for the same components in different sales, stock control and production planning files.

Much software effort was wasted in this type of file management approach. Programs were written to take account of the precise structure of files, such as the sequence of fields within records and the length of each field. If a file structure had to be altered in even a small way, like adding a field or changing the length of an existing field, all programs accessing it also had to be changed.

Database Management Systems

Special DBMSs, database management systems, were developed to overcome the limitations of file management techniques. The prime aims of a DBMS were set out in an influential report published in 1971 by the Database Task Group (DBTG) of the Codasyl Committee, an international body which also co-ordinates developments of the COBOL programming language. The basic goals of a DBMS are to:

— *avoid data duplication* by storing a data item only once, then allowing it to be associated in a variety of different relationships with other data items, depending on the application;

— *make data independent of the programs which access it*, so database structures can be altered without having to change associated programs;

— *give consistent and efficient control over long-term database developments*, for example by having a *data dictionary*, which contains full details of the database structure and knowledge of the conditions under which particular users can access certain database items.

The Codasyl DBTG provides data independence by separating the user's logical view of how information is organised in the database from the way it is stored and manipulated. The user view is defined in detailed maps (*schema*) using a *Data Description Language* (*DDL*). A *Data Manipulation Language* (*DML*) stores, retrieves and updates the actual information.

The main drawback of the DBTG recommendations is that schema, and the *subschema* which identify the data items needed for a particular application, must fully pre-define all possible relationships between data items. These are needed to help programs find their way through (*navigate*) the database, to find a specific item. When new data items are added and data relationships change, navigational paths must be redefined. Schema are also extremely complex, making them difficult for most users to understand.

A simpler, more flexible approach is based on the *relational* model, developed by IBM researcher Edgar 'Ted' Codd in the 1970s. A *Relational DBMS* (*RDBMS*) consists of many two dimensional tables whose rows and columns are equivalent, respectively, to records and fields. Relationships between items in tables are not pre-defined; they are made dynamically according to each application's needs. Increased flexibility, however, consumes more computer processing resources than DBTG schema, so performance efficiency can be a problem with relational systems.

USER DISILLUSIONMENT GROWS

DBMS developments were a response to the realisation that computer investments could be justified in the long term only by applying this powerful technology to a broad range of organisational needs. By the early 1970s, however, there was a growing sense of disillusionment about computers among managers and users. Technological promises seemed to outstrip practical results. There were many failures in implementing computer-based systems. Even the successes generally remained confined to cost-cutting and overhead tasks, rather than to the main strategic thrust of an enterprise. The few industries where computers *were* central to operations, such as airline reservations and banking, remained isolated jewels in the increasingly tarnished computer crown.

There were a number of reasons for this disillusionment: technical limitations; poor understanding of computing capabilities; constraints caused by the organisational role of DP; system design inadequacies; and software development problems.

Straining Against Technical Limitations

Mainframe batch processing systems of the 1960s could be applied successfully only to a narrow range of routine tasks. Their limitations also led to some important applications falling into disrepute. The poor quality of many management information applications had a particularly significant negative effect because it influenced general management attitudes to computers.

With batch processing, much time was spent getting information to and from the central computer room; funnelling all the computing workload through the same mainframe system also created a processing bottleneck. Reports were often difficult to read because of the rudimentary printing capabilities available at the time. (The fastest printers, for example, produced everything in capital letters on lined continuous stationery, with few capabilities to help present information attractively.) Software development problems meant that a great deal of effort was needed to create new reports or change existing ones, even for relatively small modifications.

As a result, many reports were out of date, contained incomplete information, and were too cumbersome and badly presented to be easily assimilated. Their limited value to managers and other users, or even complete irrelevance to their real needs, led not only to computer-produced reports falling into disrepute, but also seriously harmed attitudes to the DP department and computers in general.

Delays in Exploiting Innovations

There were many practical reasons why innovations that overcame early computing limitations took a long time before being incorporated widely into operational systems.

Until microelectronics began to make an impact in the mid-1970s, hardware remained relatively expensive. So, when online systems began to be available in the early 1970s, there were severe financial constraints on the number of terminals installed. The ones provided were used mainly for specialist clerical tasks (such as inputting bulk information to mainframes) rather than for daily interactions with most people from their usual work places.

Many key innovations depended on complex new software, such as DBMSs. This was at a time when software engineering was in its infancy and suppliers, as well as users, were still learning how to manage software developments successfully. Therefore, it took a long time to translate theoretical concepts into software which had acceptable levels of performance and reliability.

The cost of converting to new systems also deterred many users from introducing the latest systems. The lack of standardisation between manufacturers was further exacerbated by incompatibilities between systems within the same manufacturer's range. A move to a new system could involve the development of a completely new suite of software and the translation of all existing data into new formats. Users of communications systems were tightly locked in to the systems available from their mainframe suppliers because of the protocols supported.

This situation has eased as users of systems from larger manufacturers, particularly IBM, were offered a degree of choice due to many alternative sources of compatible systems. In hardware, *Plug-Compatible Manufacturers* (*PCMs*) began to offer systems with better price/performance, to the same standard interfaces, as the original manufacturer. Also, many suppliers began to offer systems and applications software for the more popular hardware.

Organisational Role of DP

Isolation of DP Departments

The isolation of DP departments from the rest of the organisation exacerbated a natural wariness and fear among non-specialists of a complex new technology. With little day-to-day informal contact between DP professionals and the rest of the organisation, computing experts were seen as outsiders, talking a foreign language, with the power to make significant changes to users' working lives.

The design of a computer-based information system involves the design of organisational structures, management reporting procedures, job descriptions and work routines. Computer systems designers, however, still generally view their job as primarily one of creating the best technical systems using precise 'scientific' techniques. They may give inadequate attention to the less easily quantifiable subjective and informal factors that strongly affect actual work practices, because they have insufficient practical experience of the applications they help to computerise. On the other hand, the people with expertise in business and user requirements often have too little technical knowhow to challenge the proposals made by computing specialists. This gap in understanding is a vital factor in the implementation of information management policies and still a cause of much user disillusionment.

System Ownership Problems

Another result of the isolation of DP from the rest of the organisation was that most users felt they had little say in directing developments, and so lacked a stake in ensuring they were successful. DP professionals believed their skills entitled them to be custodians of all computer systems. This belief was reinforced by the fact that a DP department was frequently the only group capable of handling negotiations with computer suppliers effectively. DP managers, therefore, usually had control of all budgets relating to any computer systems in the organisation.

At a higher organisational level, financial directors had the final say on computing investments. They naturally gave priority to systems which seemed to offer the best return on investment: in applications they understood most concretely, like financial and accounting management. Directors responsible for other key corporate functions, like marketing, sales, customer service, manufacturing, personnel and research often saw computing as being 'owned' by the finance and DP functions rather than being a corporate resource in which everyone had a stake.

The creation of a widespread sense of ownership of computer applications is, therefore, a vital factor in a successful information management strategy, and is discussed in Parts 2 and 3 of this book.

Systems Design Inadequacies

A computer-based information system must be specified in comprehensive detail before appropriate software can be written for it. Many problems have arisen in creating appropriate information systems because the design process has taken the following course:

— systems designers and analysts from the DP department have sole responsibility for producing technical designs;

— designers gather information by interviewing users and undertaking formal analyses of information flows, transactions and procedures;

— the understanding gap causes frequent misinterpretations between designers and users;

— users tend to talk in terms of traditional ways of working because they have insufficient knowledge of computing potential — systems professionals tend to think in terms of computing capabilities and working methods that best suit computers;

— having gathered the information, the designers specify the formal system that best meets their perception of user requirements;

— ambiguities, lack of formal rigour, incompatibilities and other problems in systems development methodologies cause delays and errors in producing the final system;

— the design specification is often an incomplete or incorrect interpretation even of the designer's perception of what is needed, let alone being an accurate representation of what users actually want and need;

— the system that eventually emerges relates to the static 'snapshot' of formal user requirements specified at the time the information was gathered; this could have been months or years before the operational system became available, by which time user needs could have changed substantially;

— the final system is often both an inadequate encapsulation of original users needs and is out of date;

— the process of redesigning the system begins, with similar failings.

Software Development

Software development is an intrinsically complex, error-prone task. Detailed program instructions have to be written to take account of every eventuality and must be adapted to meet continuously evolving user needs. Without effective software engineering discipline, programs can become bug-ridden — tangled webs that are difficult to construct in the first place and even harder to modify and enhance once they have become operational.

Despite disillusionment among many users, the enormous potential of computing capabilities stimulated a growing demand for new applications. Programs could be written only by skilled DP staff, who were in short supply. This caused the build up of *application backlogs*, where user requests for new systems and changes to existing ones joined long queues waiting for service from DP departments. User dissatisfaction was heightened when excuses for the consequent delays were often given in technical jargon they found incomprehensible.

The earliest programming languages employed only the binary instructions of the hardware *machine code*. The next generation of languages, called *assemblers*, used more understandable words and abbreviations but were still similar to machine code formats. Third generation languages (*3GLs*) were designed to be closer to the structures and English language words with which an application would be described naturally; they are also known as *high-level languages*.

Different high-level languages were created for various application classes, such as: COBOL (COmmon Business Oriented Language) for commercial business tasks; FORTRAN (FORmula TRANslation) for scientific software; and BASIC (Beginner's All-purpose Symbolic Instruction Code) for use in education and for newcomers to programming. Later in the 1970s, languages incorporating more structured software engineering principles, like C and Pascal (named after French mathematician Blaise Pascal), became popular for general software developments, including systems software.

INNOVATION SPURS PROGRESS

An Evolving Information Infrastructure

The various problems outlined in the previous section could have led to an inertia which confined computing to a limited business role. The quickening pace of innovation in the 1970s, however, gave a fresh impetus to the progression of computer-based information systems into more organisational activities.

Gradually, the falling costs of hardware enabled more computing facilities to be sited outside the central computer room. Data communications networks were established. Various departments and groups acquired a degree of autonomy in running their own small business systems and minicomputer-based information services. Computers were installed in ordinary offices. The convergence into IT led to the divergence of applications discussed in Chapter 1. Smaller organisations also began to rely more on computers. Over time, organisations developed an *infrastructure* of computer systems, often in an *ad hoc* way. Frequently, there were significant incompatibilities between the hardware, software, files, databases and data communications facilities employed in different parts of the organisation, or with different applications. The infrastructure was often like a curate's egg — good in parts. Some systems were highly successful, others were failures. All had to be considered when planning future developments.

An existing IT infrastructure represents more than just an investment in hardware and software, although that in itself is substantial. Its development and use also creates an investment in expertise and technical skills for the particular systems and methods of working involved. Large costs in systems conversion, re-training and re-learning have to be faced when making changes to substantial elements in the infrastructure. Many organisations have, therefore, lived for a long time with the infrastructures that evolved from the 1970s, or even earlier.

Moving Up the Learning Curve

The speed of innovation in IT has continued to go faster than most people, including technical specialists, can assimilate. People and organisations have to go through a practical learning process of gaining experience with, and confidence in a technology, before they can make rapid progress in exploiting capabilities fully. This is known as moving along a *learning curve*.

At first, a relatively long time is taken to learn how to do basic tasks, often with a great deal of trial and error. The pace of learning increases once there is more familiarity with the technology, particularly if tangible benefits have been provided to whet the appetite for more sophisticated applications. Many organisations proceeded along the learning curve as part of the historical evolution of IT. They started slowly with DP. This experience helped in the next phase of distributed computing. In the 1980s, after almost two decades of slow and, at times, painful learning, there has been a rapid escalation up the learning curve towards more advanced, integrated computer-based information systems.

Even organisations that moved to computers much later needed to go through a similar process, although they may have benefited from lessons learnt by others and had the ability to start from scratch in building an infrastructure based on the latest technology. The corporate culture, management style, working routines and strategies of each organisation are unique. Time is needed to learn how the complexities and power of IT can be applied most appropriately in a particular environment, but new enterprises that build a computer strategy into their basic corporate plan from the beginning may be able to progress more quickly to sophisticated applications.

For individuals, gaining direct experience and benefits from IT is an important element in moving up the learning curve. Many managers, for example, began to appreciate the real extent of what could be achieved with IT only when they started using their own PCs. This gave them a practical feel for the power and flexibility of computing, which was difficult to grasp from more indirect contacts with the technology. Many managers were first attracted to PCs by easy-to-use *spreadsheet* software which enable planning models to be built and manipulated. They display grids of rows and columns (the 'spreadsheet') on a screen. Elements in the model and relationships between them, such as factors that contribute to a departmental budget, are input by users. Once a spreadsheet has been set up, it can help to advise users what would happen if various factors change, such as costs or sales.

Having experienced the value of spreadsheets, managers began to explore other PC software. Some did their own programming because the easiest to use high-level language, BASIC, is available on most PCs. Many other people, at all levels in the organisation, gained direct personal experience of IT through PCs, word processors, terminals and various workstations.

Expanding Beyond Traditional DP Constraints

As organisations built their computing infrastructure and moved up the IT learning curve, the business focus of applications gradually broadened. Initially, the main targets were to cut costs and administrative overheads, as typified by DP systems. Then interest was shown in the provision of information to help management decision-making and control. The evolving pervasiveness of IT through more and more activities made computer-based information systems a key corporate resource for adding value to products, customer service and other strategic issues fundamental to corporate success and survival. This began to include direct links to suppliers, dealers, retail outlets, banks and other external organisations.

The availability of low-cost PCs and word processors gave many managers the motivation and opportunity to take more direct control over their own computing resources. They provided immediate, tangible benefits to their local operations. Their price was also sufficiently low to fall below the levels which needed to be approved by the DP department.

In some organisations, this led to an unco-ordinated spread of many small computer systems. They were generally obtained for specific short-term needs, which they often achieved satisfactorily. Little attention was paid, however, to compatibility with other systems in the organisation, or longer-term growth potential. Much time and money was wasted because of this and the lack of experience in selecting and managing computers. There was also substantial duplication of effort in learning about and implementing a variety of systems with overlapping features. Nevertheless, many users found the responsiveness of their own systems a great improvement on the delays and frustrations caused when everything had to be channelled through a central corporate computing service.

IT convergence also propelled computing across many management boundaries. Word processors and other computer-based office systems were seen to fall under the responsibility of office administrators. Computer networks and computerised telephone exchanges were regarded by telephone and communications managers as part of their own spheres of influence. Computer-aided design and manufacturing often came under the responsibility of production departments.

Helping Users Develop Their Own Systems

Attempts have been made to cope with the applications backlog by providing tools that can be used by non-specialist users to develop their own applications. These new approaches became known as *Fourth Generation Languages* (4GLs) to indicate the move beyond third generation languages like COBOL, used exclusively by DP specialists. The earliest of the new software development aids were *report generators*, which allow users to create and manipulate report formats easily.

Subsequently 4GLs have become more sophisticated and powerful. They enable reasonably complex programs to be expressed in the language and concepts that are natural to the application concerned.

Many 4GL operations involve carrying out tasks using a database, therefore many advanced user-oriented *applications development tools* are integrated with a DBMS. Relational DBMSs, in particular, were specifically designed to be easily manipulated by non-specialist users. For example, *query languages* (of which *Structured Query Language* (*SQL*) is the most widely available) enable users to request information from a DBMS as they want it, without having to pre-define all queries in, say, a COBOL program.

Some DP departments have set up *information centres* outside the traditional DP environments to provide support and training geared to help users solve more of their own computing needs. Personal computers, 4GLs, word processors, spreadsheets and other systems are made available in information centres to give users hands-on experience of their capabilities, assisted by specialist staff who can 'talk the user's language'. Information centres attempt to balance the desire of users to gain greater control over their own systems with the need to maximise overall exploitation of corporate computing investment and expertise. Their management and operation are examined in Chapter 12.

INTEGRATION INTO CORPORATE STRATEGIES

Bridging Islands of Automation

The *ad hoc* evolution of various information systems in an organisation has created a number of *islands of automation*. The main islands cover broad organisational functions, each of which has its own traditions, culture, management style, staff motivation and technical requirements.

The Office

Office automation has been applied to work characterised by relatively informal human interaction and working patterns, with very low rates of previous technological innovation. Information in office filing and communications systems is far less structured than in traditional DP applications. Much office information is in the form of text and documents, which need fundamentally different approaches to being stored, searched, processed and analysed than structured DP data. Office staff also expect a far greater degree of variety and discretion in their jobs than has been common on production lines, where 'automation' practices were developed first (discussed in Chapter 3).

Manufacturing

Manufacturing automation has roots which go beyond the advent of computers as frequent technical innovation has taken place on production lines. Product design offices, however, are closer in practice to traditional office management methods than shop-floor approaches. Within the manufacturing function, different types of automation have been applied at different times; so there are often separate manufacturing islands within the overall operation.

Telecommunications

Telecommunications involve an amalgam of various traditional approaches, such as the telephone, telex and mail room. Managers responsible for a company's telephone network have generally taken increasing responsibility for computer-based networks without realising that fundamentally new technical skills are needed. Conversely, truly networked information systems pose technical challenges significantly different to those for which DP staff were traditionally trained.

Promoting Connectivity

As has been previously indicated, many DP islands have evolved, ranging from mainframe corporate DP systems, through departmental systems, to a plethora of PCs, often obtained without DP co-ordination. Different databases, software, networks, workstations, terminals and other DP systems may be operating in separate organisational activities. The integration of these islands of automation, and 'sub-islands' within them, is an essential stage in integrating information systems. That is why General Motors, Boeing and many other users are playing a leading role in developing standards like OSI, which promote more systems *connectivity*.

Connectivity is required at various levels between different processors, workstations, terminals, software tools, applications, databases and networks. Connections may need to be made to systems in other organisations, as well as across internal departmental systems.

DP Transmutes into IS

Within the diversity of IT developments, DP has become just one computer application among many. The co-ordination of computer-based systems has increasingly become the responsibility of a function at a higher organisational level than DP departments, variously called

Information Systems (*IS*), *Information Processing* (*IP*), *Management Information Services* (*MIS*) or other titles that stress *information* rather than *data* applications. The IS division or department will be responsible for some, but not all, systems in the organisation. However, increasing emphasis is being placed on making users the owners of their own information systems, even if much of the associated hardware is in the IS division's *data centre*, the name commonly used for the facility housing the main corporate hardware, including mainframes.

The IS function has the task of integrating all information systems around common information management policies, as illustrated in Figure 2.1. The basis of this is the IS infrastructure, which consists of more than just the relevant IT tools. It also includes the appropriate IS management strategy to ensure there is effective co-ordination and support for all corporate and local user needs. The way in which the IS function is translated into specific organisational structures and management responsibilities will vary between organisations (see Chapter 6). Key elements that should form the basis of all IS strategies include:

— The IS function must be integral to top-level management decision-making processes.

— The IS function must integrate and co-ordinate IS developments while leaving ultimate ownership and direction of business systems under the control of relevant users.

LOOKING OUTWARDS

The business focus of information systems has moved from an inward concentration on internal organisational efficiencies to systems that reach outwards towards clients, customers, suppliers and other organisations and individuals. Many information systems now span the globe and a multitude of organisations and users.

The initial step was generally to provide links to customers and direct business associates. Banks' ATMs (Automated Teller Machines) were the first obvious example. Now, it is also possible to access an organisation's information systems via home-based videotex and other services, eg to order goods, or interact with your bank account. Links to suppliers, retailers, agents, dealers, and so on, help to give many organisations a competitive advantage.

Global information networks have made a fundamental change to

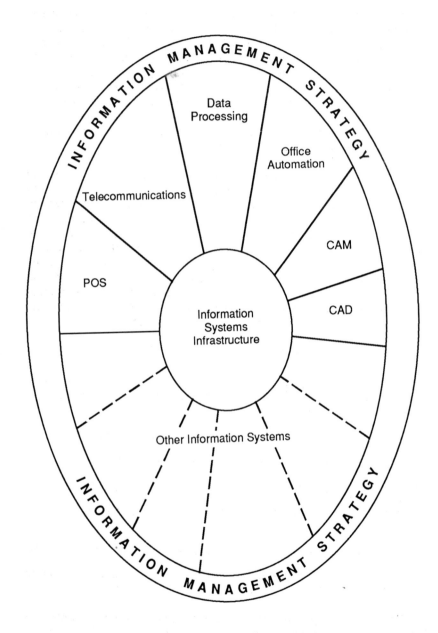

Figure 2.1   The Integrated Information System (IS) Function

many industries. For example, dealings in equities, foreign exchanges, commodities and other financial services are generally handled via round-the-world, round-the-clock computer-based information systems. Another example is the shipping industry which has drastically modified traditional ways of working using *Electronic Data Interchange (EDI)* systems that enable information to be transmitted electronically between exporters/importers, agents, transportation operators and others in the shipment chain. This cuts the need for a great deal of paperwork and the errors which inevitably occur when information is being handled manually by so many different people.

As more links grow between organisations, the structure of industries changes. This has happened in the shipping industry because EDI has reduced, even eliminated, the need for a number of intermediary activities between the sending and receipt of goods. The information system can itself become an important bargaining point in competitive power battles within industry. A particularly successful information system can help to tie-in various suppliers and agents to the company that owns the system; or access can be denied to certain information systems if some groups in an industry feel it would give a few companies an unfair advantage. Information systems are, therefore, key strategic elements within many industries and market sectors.

SUMMARY: PARTNERSHIPS FOR SUCCESS

This chapter has explained how business information systems have evolved within organisations and industries. Success is most likely to be achieved with IT when:

— IS direction is regarded as a top management function;

— all information systems are co-ordinated effectively;

— an efficient and flexible IS infrastructure is established;

— information systems are 'owned' by users who feel they have a stake in their success;

— IS developments are responsive to changing user and business needs;

— time is allowed for systems to progress at an evolutionary pace along the natural learning curve.

Any one IS project is likely to involve many different people and groups within an organisation. IS developments must, therefore, be managed as a *partnership* between managers, users and IS professionals.

The forging of such partnerships depends on the skill with which management creates an organisational culture that promotes positive attitudes to information systems, supported by widespread understanding of the practical business potential and limitations of IT.

3 The Management Context

TURNING TECHNOLOGY-PUSH INTO USER-PULL

Many IS developments have been propelled by a *technological imperative:* the desire to 'do something' with a new technology. In this environment, user and business requirements tend to follow the route determined by innovative technological directions.

The traditional role of DP specialists, highlighted in Chapter 2, reinforced the technology push behind computing applications. DP professionals were the prime instigators of developments and generally controlled most computing investments. Non-specialist managers and users generally had insufficient knowledge and skills to challenge the jargon-rich proposals put forward by DP departments.

A common problem in these circumstances was an over-emphasis on the optimum potential of the technology, while its practical limitations were underplayed until they hit against the bedrock of reality. Computing enthusiasts and suppliers have frequently combined to 'hype' a capability that is still in a prototype or testing phase. In practice, it has taken many years before the potential has been fulfilled in reliable working systems. For example, DBMSs were first mooted in the late 1960s, but it took at least a decade before suitable products were on the market and a body of expertise had been built up to make their application feasible in a large number of activities. Many other capabilities have followed a similar pattern of high early promise, followed by a lengthy period of development and learning before the claimed benefits became reality on a wide scale.

The effective harnessing of technological potential depends on a realistic understanding of what new systems can deliver and an ability to target developments at well-chosen user and business goals. The increasing involvement of general management in taking responsibility for IS applications is helping more organisations to achieve this. Technology-push is turning into user-pull. However, simply giving users more responsibility cannot, in itself, ensure that full business benefits are gained from computer-based information systems. Broader management methods also have a decisive influence.

ACHIEVING ORGANISATIONAL SUCCESS

In an attempt to improve national and business economic performance, many governments, commentators and suppliers have used the slogan *automate or die*. Unfortunately, it is also possible to automate *and* die. The same hardware, software or communications systems, applied to similar functions, can succeed in one company or department but fail in another. The reasons lie in the nature of the organisational environment within which the system is developed, implemented and operated. This environment grows from a corporate culture consisting of the particular management style, organisational structures, staff attitudes and working procedures that characterise the enterprise as a whole, or particular groups within it. Information management has become an intrinsic part of the culture: influenced by it and also changing it.

The plans for an information system, for example, may include the design of:

— *organisational structures* such as: which departments exist, their areas of responsibility, and how they interact with each other;

— *reporting and communications pathways* between: managers and subordinates, individuals at varying levels in the organisation, corporate and local management, geographically dispersed locations, outside organisations, customers, etc;

— *jobs*: including scope of responsibility, tasks performed, degree of autonomy allowed, skills required, and opportunities for career development;

— *administrative procedures* to be followed.

Many information systems fail because insufficient attention is given to these organisational and human impacts, resulting in systems that are inadequately tuned to the nuances and needs of the working environments in which they are used. Resistance to a system can be caused if those affected by it have not been part of the process of creating it. Changes are more likely to be accepted if they are seen to fit a rationale that has evolved from a genuine understanding of the traditional organisational culture and show tangible benefits to individuals, groups and the organisation as a whole.

THE ROOTS OF MODERN MANAGEMENT METHODS

Historical Background

Early Egyptian, Babylonian and Chinese civilisations established sophisticated systems for planning, organising and controlling military, industrial and commercial enterprises. Grecian civilisation introduced systematic techniques of research, analysis and scholarship which could be applied to many aspects of society, including management. Xenophon, one of Socrates' disciples, for example, wrote extensively about management principles which could be applied to any activity.

In the fifteenth and sixteenth centuries, the flourishing maritime trade centred on Venice led to the creation of new forms of business organisation and control. These included well-documented procedures and standards for the efficient and reliable control of accounting, stock movements, assembly-line production, warehousing and costs.

The industrial revolution of the eighteenth century caused rapid progress away from an agrarian economy. Radical new management practices were needed to steer and organise emerging industrial enterprises. For example, Sir Richard Arkwright, inventor of the spinning frame, built a successful business using innovative and efficient management principles, such as organising factories to provide continuous production, dividing the labour process into specialised functions, carefully planning the siting of plants and generally co-ordinating the use of machines, materials, people and money.

In 1800, a company set up to manufacture James Watt's steam engine built the Soho Engineering foundry based on what were then advanced management techniques. These included the layout of machines to produce the most efficient work flow, adjustments to machine speeds to produce optimum work throughput, the use of piece-rate payments as an incentive to workers, market forecasting, and other applications of scientifically-controlled planning.

The Rise of Rationalism

The industrial revolution was part of a movement which placed increasing stress on the application of rational thought and analysis to solving a wide variety of human, technical and scientific problems. Eighteenth century writers like Adam Smith and Jeremy Bentham formulated these ideas into the *rationalist* philosophies, which provided an impetus to the growth of management and organisation theories.

The basic premise of rationalism was that the 'objective', logical methods of research, classification and quantification used by Sir Isaac Newton to unravel the laws of physics can also help to find underlying universal principles which determine the behaviour of social and economic systems. The rationalists believed human happiness could be maximised by applying these principles to organising, managing and running government and business enterprises.

Two centuries later, the widespread use of computers in most aspects of modern society provided a powerful tool to implement rationalist ideology because computers operate on strictly logical procedures. It is therefore not surprising that Charles Babbage saw the development between 1821 and 1859 of his *calculating engines* as an important stage in the industrial revolution. They would, he predicted in 1851, lead to the "substitution of machinery not merely for the skill of the human hand, but for the relief of the human intellect."

The next year, Babbage published *On the Economy of Machinery and Manufactures* in which he described how the 'principles of generalisation' he had employed in developing calculating engines could be applied to managing business enterprises. He recommended that information should be gathered, ie by the use of a stop watch, on precisely how long it took to perform different work tasks. He believed jobs should be organised to encourage specialisation in the work force. He wrote that:

> "The constant repetition of the same process necessarily produces in the workman a degree of excellence and rapidity in his department, which is never possessed by a person who is obliged to execute many different processes."

Many of Babbage's management ideas became the backbone of twentieth century manufacturing automation, although they are now more usually associated with *Taylorism*, named after Frederick Winslow Taylor, an American engineer who has been a seminal influence on modern management practices.

Scientific Management Takes Centre Stage

In the late nineteenth century, increasing attention was given to defining and improving the management function because of the sudden expansion of large commercial enterprises, such as banks and railroads. A number of independent strains of management thinking began to evolve in different countries. For example, in Germany, Georg Siemens, head of the Deutsche Bank, examined the role of top management and the problems of communicating information in large organisations. In Japan, statesman and business leader Eiichi Shibusawa looked at the relations between business and national goals, and between business needs and individual ethics. In America, Henry Towne, President of the Yale and Towne Manufacturing Company, presented his paper *The Engineer as an Economist* in 1886 to the American Society of Mechanical Engineers. It called for the recognition of a 'science of management' and raised key management issues he believed should be investigated and resolved in the future.

In the same year, Taylor joined this Society and heard Towne's paper. Taylor took up Towne's challenge by developing his theory of *scientific management*, now known as Taylorism. He was particularly interested in the 'science' of systematic observation and measurement of work tasks — the kind of *time and motion* studies also advocated by Babbage.

Taylor said managers should be the 'planners' and 'thinkers' who could achieve maximum prosperity for their employers and employees by a combination of scientific work organisation, quantified production targets and a workforce which is well rewarded when it achieves its production targets. Building on the tradition of the division of labour that had evolved during the industrial revolution, he broke jobs into small isolated units, each requiring only a limited range of specialised skills. Task efficiency could be calculated using stop watches to determine their optimum duration.

Taylor expected overall work organisation to be rationalised to ensure all individual tasks are integrated to give maximum total productivity throughput. He sought to reduce or eliminate unpredictable elements from the system — particularly variable human behaviour. Therefore, he recommended that workers should follow predetermined tasks with little or no chance to exercise discretion in choosing how or when to do a task. In order to optimise task performance and worker rewards, Taylor said staff should be selected scientifically to match the tasks they were to perform and be trained to improve their specialist skills.

Taylor also introduced specialisation into managerial jobs through the concept of *functional management*. One of these functions, Taylor suggested, should be a separate planning unit. He also pioneered *management by exception* techniques through the idea of producing reports for managers that highlight exceptions from past performance and planned norms.

In 1914, Taylorism achieved its first major real-world recognition when it formed the basis for the machine-paced assembly line at the Ford motor car factory in Michigan, USA. After that, it became popular throughout the world, in capitalist and communist societies. For example, from the 1920s, the Soviet Union officially promoted the 'scientific organisation of labour', known as NOT (Nauchnaya Organizatsiya Tuda) and based on many of Taylor's principles.

Analysing How Organisations Function

In the late nineteenth century, a Germany philosopher, Max Weber, was interested in how authority may be established when science and rationalism takes over from religion as the dominant power in society. His research led him to develop models of 'authority structures' which have been strongly influential on management studies of the formal characteristics of organisations.

Weber defined three main types of organisation. In *charismatic* ones, authority relies on the personality of individuals, such as the founder of a company. In *traditional* organisations the authority is based on past custom and practice. The third type of organisation in Weber's classification, the *rational-legal bureaucracy,* is the one he saw as becoming an integral part of any industrial society, whether based on capitalist or socialist principles.

In these bureaucracies, the goals of the organisation are defined by a rational analysis of what is trying to be achieved. Authority is exercised through rules and procedures that establish the 'legality' of particular actions. Weber's concept of 'bureaucracy' has very different connotations to today's use of the term, which often implies considerable administrative inefficiency. He said rational-legal bureaucracies had qualities of "precision, speed, unambiguity, knowledge of files, continuity, discretion, strict subordination and reduction of friction and of material and personal costs..." which makes them technically superior to any other form of organisation.

In the light of current IS developments, it is interesting to note that Weber's bureaucratic model is based on a 'bureau' for the safe keeping of all written information and the explicit definition of a set of rules and procedures which theoretically provide for all eventualities. These elements have been translated into computer-based systems as databases and software that automatically program the implementation of rational-legal procedures.

Defining the Management Function

In 1916, the French mining engineer Henri Fayol published a paper which provided a comprehensive analysis of management activities, on a broader basis than Taylor's focus on how managers organise work. Fayol defined five key elements in the role of management:

— *planning*: forecasting future developments, setting objectives, formulating policies, analysing problems, and establishing action plans;

— *organising*: building the organisational structure, determining what activities are necessary to achieve objectives, ensuring appropriate human and other resources are available to carry them out satisfactorily, and classifying work, dividing it up and assigning it to groups and individuals;

— *commanding*: ensuring staff work effectively to achieve the purposes of the organisation;

— *controlling*: checking performance against the plans, seeing that actual working methods conform to established rules and expressed commands;

— *co-ordinating*: binding together, unifying and harmonising all activity and effort.

Fayol also defined a number of principles which he recommended managers should use to carry out their functions successfully. These included a strict hierarchical system of authority, with each person having only one boss. He urged managers to provide leadership that encourages individual initiatives and fairness in business practices, which he defined as a combination of 'kindliness and justice'. He also incorporated some of Taylor's ideas, such as specialisation in the division of work and the use of financial rewards as an important motivator.

Some of Fayol's ideas are regarded by many modern managers as too authoritarian and inflexible because of his emphasis on management by 'commandment', rather than consent, and his strict adherence to top-down hierarchical structures. Nevertheless, Fayol's definitions and principles have provided the solid theoretical groundwork for subsequent developments in *management sciences*.

Work Study Developments

Taylorism led directly to the establishment of the management science discipline of *Work Study*. (Work Study specialists even talk about

'BT' for Before Taylor.) Between the world wars, Taylor-based Work Study methods became the prime basis for manufacturing automation throughout the world. When Work Study techniques were applied to office tasks, they became known as *Organisation and Methods* (*O&M*).

Organisation and Methods includes studies into managerial, reporting and communications structures and responsibilities within an organisation, as well as clerical task-design and the application of time and motion methods to clerical jobs. It also involves *systems analysis* techniques, such as the use of *flowcharts* to specify, in diagrammatic form, activities and procedures of an existing or proposed organisation or work system. O&M is closely associated with computing developments, particularly its systems analysis approach.

Another management science with its roots pre-First World War is *Operations* (or *Operational*) *Research* (*OR*). It combines a variety of disciplines, such as applied mathematics, statistical analysis, probability theory and accounting, to create logical models of the behaviour of large systems involving the interaction of people, machines, materials and money. Quantified measures of elements in the model and their relationships with each other are used to assess the risks and likely success of alternative decisions, strategies and controls.

OR initially emerged as a coherent science from military operations. In the First World War for example, Thomas A Edison used statistical analyses to help American ships evade and destroy submarines. In the Second World War, OR and 'operations analysis' groups were set up in Britain and the USA. They were successful in improving many crucial activities, such as early-warning radar, anti-aircraft gunnery and determining optimum sizes of merchant shipping convoys. After the war, OR was accepted as an intrinsic part of management sciences.

How OR Helps Computerisation

A number of OR methodologies have been developed which are ideally suited for use in computer software. The following are some of the most popular of these:

> *Modelling and simulation.* The basic OR tool is the creation of models, using mathematical and statistical analyses, which can predict the probable outcome of alternative courses of action or simulate the behaviour of complex systems.

> *Queuing theory.* This evolved from work at the Dutch Post Office

in about 1910 to predict the size of telephone exchanges needed to handle current and future demand. It is now a sophisticated mathematical solution to a variety of problems, including scheduling systems, traffic control, designing the layout and staffing of supermarkets to ensure there are sufficient customer service points, multi-user systems software and telecommunications network management.

Stock control. Models for working out optimum economic and operational stock levels have been available since 1915. Sophisticated statistical methods for forecasting and controlling inventory are now in general use.

Cost-benefit analyses. By quantifying investment factors according to a common scale, usually money-based, systematic techniques have been developed to calculate the size and time scales of likely costs and benefits (see Chapter 8). Many of these rely on OR developments.

Project management. Henry Gantt, a contemporary and protégé of Taylor, developed a graphical means of representing the sub-tasks that go to form a complete project, such as constructing a building, or controlling a production line. In the 1950s, these *Gantt charts* were refined to produce *network diagrams* representing the component elements of a system using project management techniques called *Critical Path Analysis* (*CPA*) and *Program Evaluation and Review Technique* (*PERT*).

Network analyses. CPA, PERT and other network analysis techniques can be applied to many problems other than project management, such as in finding an optimum route between points in a network, as when scheduling vehicle movements between depots or in finding pathways through communications networks.

Decision theory. All OR techniques are in some way concerned with helping people, particularly managers, to make decisions. In the 1950s and 60s, social and systems scientists, like Norbert Wiener and Herbert Simon in the USA and Stafford Beer in Britain, developed more comprehensive and subtle models of how organisations behave and decisions are made. This is known as *cybernetics*. OR provides some of the basic tools for cybernetics and other decision sciences.

Linear and dynamic programming. The term 'programming' is often used in OR to describe particular mathematical techniques. *Linear programming* deals with problems containing variables, say x and y, whose relationships are expressed in equations that avoid any multiplication of the variables, such as xy or y^2, so that they can be expressed graphically as a straight line. It is used, for instance, to calculate the optimum mix of a product's ingredients to maximise profits or to decide which factories should supply which warehouse to minimise transportation costs. *Dynamic programming* is a logical procedure by which a sequence of choices can be made where each choice is between two or more possibilities, such as deciding when and how many items of equipment to replace (say, the vehicles in a car hire firm).

A More Human-centred Approach

The scientific management developments discussed so far generally take a mechanistic view of how organisations function, work is performed, decisions are made and other management issues. In fact, Weber described rational-legal bureaucracies as 'organisational machines'.

Another view of management and organisations has also developed, which gives more emphasis to the human and social behavioural aspects of organisations. It is more interested in qualitative factors, subjective perceptions and the generally imprecise, variable and unpredictable behaviour of individuals and groups. It has had strong impacts on modern management ideas, but is much less amenable to direct computerisation than scientific management theories.

Scottish industrialist Robert Owen set up small factories in New Lanark in 1820 which sowed the seeds of this new approach. He sought to improve manufacturing productivity by paying as much attention to the welfare of workers, on and off the job, as to the machines which had driven the industrial revolution. However, it took many years before New Lanark ceased being an isolated example of more human-centred management techniques.

In 1910, a German-born professor of experimental psychology at Harvard University, Hugo Muensterberg, began research in the application of psychology to industry. He saw industrial psychology as being complementary to Taylorism by helping to find workers best suited to particular tasks and to find out the psychological conditions that produce the greatest output per worker. Henry Gantt called for Taylorism to be adapted to policies that consider an individual's needs, for example, by seeking to teach and instruct workers, rather than drive them down pre-planned routes.

Co-operating Towards Common Goals

An important new perspective on the operation of organisations was provided by the writings of Mary Parker Follet, particularly during the 1920s. She was born in Boston and educated at Harvard and Cambridge universities in philosophy, history and political sciences. As a social worker in Boston, she helped develop youth employment bureaux, which started her interest in industry and management.

Follet dealt with questions of organisation, leadership and power as essentially human problems. She argued that management's prime aim should be to weld a partnership that ensures the overall goals of an organisation are also the common aims of each individual and group within it. She proposed four fundamental organisational principles to create an 'integrative unity' where everyone is brought to a natural realisation of what has to be done. Follet's principles are:

Co-ordinate by having the people responsible for an activity in direct contact with each other. This makes *horizontal communication* across the organisation as important as *vertical* chains of command in achieving co-ordination.

Involve all those concerned with a policy or decision in the early stages while policies are being formulated. Follet believed this would increase morale, motivation and commitment to the goals when established.

Explicitly examine all relevant factors and the relationships between them, including joint fact-finding studies and open discussion of differences.

Regard co-ordination as a continuing process in which an executive decision is a 'moment in a process'. So many people contribute to this decision-making process, according to Follet, that conclusions should be regarded as arising from combined knowledge and joint responsibility.

The goals of co-operation and consensus, with widespread input to decision-making, have become part of many modern management styles, such as in modern Japanese industry. The Japanese notion of *quality circles*, for example, systematically elicits the views of all those concerned with particular activities as part of an integrated corporate-wide strategy to develop appropriate policies and work procedures.

In the 1960s, the prolific management writer Peter Drucker popularised his theory of *management by objectives*, which he saw as a systematic means of creating integrated corporate goals and of motivating managers. He said executives should be responsible for setting a broad range of objectives in their own areas of authority. They should also be provided with information to help them judge their performance against these objectives. He sees management as a group activity, but with objectives that relate each manager's contribution to corporate performance. The result, according to Drucker, will enhance co-ordination, co-operation and motivation.

Formal and Informal Organisations

By emphasising the value of direct co-operation between many individuals and groups, irrespective of their position in hierarchical organisation structures, Follet highlighted the existence of important *informal* groupings and lines of communication within the formal structure.

Between 1927 and 1932, Elton Mayo, an Australian-born Professor of Industrial Research at Harvard University, conducted a series of studies at the Hawthorne works of Western Electric Company in Chicago which provided evidence of the role played by this 'informal organisation'. Mayo's Hawthorne experiment examined the attitudes and reactions of groups of workers operating under various conditions. He found that working methods depended more on informal social group interactions than the physical environment in which work takes place.

Mayo's work focused on the role of work groups. Chester I Barnard, who was President of the New Jersey Bell Telephone Company for many years from 1927, examined the broader relationship between formal and informal organisations. He defined formal organisations in terms of communications between many people who contribute actions towards a common purpose. Informal organisations, on the other hand, derive from interactions between people based on personal goals, he said. Barnard foresaw a continual interaction between formal and informal organisations. He believed formal organisations, particularly in large enterprises, are effective only if they make explicit many informal attitudes and traditions. However, he warned that even successful enterprises could become fossilised unless new informal organisations were allowed to develop. The informal organisation gives individuals a degree of personal choice in their local sphere, helps personal motivation and enables operations to be adjusted to local circumstances. He said these informal benefits cannot be adequately catered for within the formal organisation that exists at a particular time.

In the 1970s and 80s, French sociologist Michel Crozier argued that computers could limit the ability of large organisations to make vital *ad hoc* adjustments to local needs because formal organisational procedures may be programmed into software that enforce automatic conformance to these rules.

Managing the Human Factor

Mayo's efforts to build a better understanding and awareness of the human factor in work situations helped stimulate *human relations* and *industrial sociology* management studies. These examine what motivates individuals and groups.

American psychologist Frederick Herzberg led pioneering research work in the 1950s and 60s into human motivation at work and its effects on an individual's psychological growth and mental health. His major finding was to distinguish between *motivational* factors, which give a positive sense of job satisfaction, and *hygiene* factors, which can prevent dissatisfaction but contribute relatively little to feelings of personal fulfilment at work. Herzberg's five main motivators are: achievement, recognition, the attraction of the work itself, responsibility, and advancement. Hygiene factors include: salary, supervision, company administration, interpersonal relationships, and working conditions. Hygiene factors must be provided to satisfactory levels, otherwise they will cause dissatisfaction.

In order to avoid motivators becoming vague 'good intentions', Herzberg developed a systematic approach to job design which differed radically from Taylorism's rationalisation into specialised and simplified tasks. Instead, Herzberg defined principles of *job enrichment* that encourage the provision of adequate motivators for individuals. This, he said, could be achieved by defining jobs that offer: a variety of opportunities for exercising discretion in the timing and method of carrying out tasks; allocation of complete natural units of work to individuals; gradually granting increased authority to individuals in performing their job; and introducing new and more difficult tasks over a period of time.

In the 1960s, American social psychologist Douglas McGregor examined how different management styles were based on distinct perceptions of human behaviour. The traditional approach, typified by the recommendations of Taylor and Fayol, assume what McGregor called *Theory X:* that the average person intrinsically dislikes work, prefers to be directed, wishes to avoid responsibility and, above all, wants security. This results in management by authoritarian direction, control and coercion. McGregor proposed an alternative *Theory Y*: that most people do not inherently dislike work, respond well if offered opportunities to take responsibility and have a creative contribution to make in solving problems at work. This leads to management based on co-operation and the integration of corporate and individual needs, as typified in the work of Follet, Mayo, Herzberg and others.

In 1981, William Ouchi defined *Theory Z* as the group of successful Japanese industrial approaches, such as management by consensus, quality circles and job rotation.

Socio-technical Organisation and Work Design

A group of social psychologists at the Tavistock Institute of Human Relations in London has developed a method of systems design which seeks to resolve the often conflicting requirements of social, technical and economic aspects of an organisation or work situation. The approach was initially developed from a project in 1949 for the British National Coal Board (now British Coal) into the impact of new technology on work practices and miners' motivation.

Mining mechanisation had made it possible to work on a single long coal face (*longwall*) rather than a series of shorter faces. Despite the potential for higher efficiency from the new techniques, low morale and low productivity had generally followed the switch to longwall working. The Tavistock team, led by Eric Trist, discovered that major problems arose because of the way work had been organised in response to increased mechanisation. With short faces, work was based on a small group carrying out complete tasks, with the group having considerable autonomy in deciding how to complete their work satisfactorily. The longwall method had led to the organisation of work as if it were a factory production line, with little contact between individuals, who generally worked in isolation or as part of a small clique.

A colliery in South Yorkshire, however, was achieving great success with a different form of work organisation. Instead of having the mines organised in shift groups, with each shift responsible for a different task, and no communication or shared responsibility between groups, miners at this colliery had gone back to working in small groups. Each of these groups took responsibility for the entire work cycle of part of a face and allowed considerable freedom in deciding how to achieve their targets. Research into how this could be successfully applied in other collieries led Trist to develop the concept of an organisation or work system consisting of interdependent social and technical aspects.

This *socio-technical* approach aims to optimise overall effectiveness by explicitly considering social and psychological factors, as well as the technological and economic ones that dominate scientific management. It recognises the dynamic nature of organisations and their functioning. Socio-technical work design principles favour: integrating separate tasks into complete work units; multi-skilled jobs; group working; discretionary rather than prescribed work roles; self-regulation rather than excessive control and supervision by superiors; and increasing variety and autonomy at work. Many of these are direct opposites to basic tenets of Taylorism.

One of Trist's work design principles is particularly relevant to information systems: people should be treated as complementary to, not as extensions of, or being subservient to, machines and new technology.

Ergonomic Comfort and Efficiency

Robert Owen recognised that improvements to the quality of the working environment can improve overall work efficiency by increasing worker motiviation. Taylor, on the other hand, studied the layout and design of factories primarily in terms of economic efficiency. Ergonomic and human factors engineering research seeks to balance human, technical and economic factors in the physical design of workplaces and the interaction between users and machines.

The design of consumer products has long recognised the importance of producing equipment that can be used without a great deal of prior training or high risks of error during use. For example, considerable care, including extensive measurements of human physiology, was used in designing early telephone handsets. The application of ergonomics to more complex technologies started in the Second World War, including a study by the US Air Force into designing aircraft controls to eliminate pilot error.

In manufacturing plants, mines, and other potentially dangerous working environments, ergonomics focused on health and safety issues. In offices, ergonomics initially concentrated mainly on physical aspects, such as the design of chairs, desks, lighting, heating, etc.

In computing, ergonomic concerns first focused on the physical design of VDUs. There are now clear-cut guidelines which will give adequate operator comfort and health protection, provided they are used in appropriate environments and with working practices that avoid causing stress and anxiety. The interest in VDU ergonomics has broadened into more general issues of user/system interaction and job design. Chapters 2 and 9 discuss human factors engineering in computer-based man-machine interfaces in more detail.

Strategic Management Becomes Topical

During the 1970s and 80s, management and business studies have proliferated. There have been various trends and fads, often stimulated by best-selling books. Many of the ideas, theories and recommendations that have emerged are based on trying to draw lessons from an analysis of actual managerial experience and case studies, particularly in larger organisations. (References to some of the most influential books and articles are given in Appendix 2.)

One of the trends has been concerned with *quality management*. It was stimulated in the US by observations of how Japanese industry had been so successful by seeking to eliminate faults in products at their source, through systematic quality control procedures. With slogans like 'right, first time, every time' and detailed monitoring and measurement of the reduction of defects and improvement in performance, this movement has focused a variety of management methods on quality goals. (Chapter 7 discusses quality management further in relation to information systems.)

At a broader level, an important influence on modern management studies was the book *Strategy and Structure* by business historian Alfred Chandler, published in 1962. *Strategy* is the definition of long-term objectives and the formulation and implementation of detailed plans to achieve them. *Structure* is the organisation built to administer and support the strategies. Chandler, using a number of detailed case studies of major American corporations, said that structure follows from the strategy adopted.

Chandler helped to establish strategic management as an important priority. However, some of Chandler's ideas and theories have been refined and challenged by others. Management and organisation specialist Harold Leavitt, for instance, defines tasks, people, environment, and information and control as the key influences on organisation dynamics, in addition to structure. And while working at management consultants McKinsey and Co, Thomas J Peters and Robert H Waterman Jr helped to define the *McKinsey 7-S Framework* in which strategy, structure, systems, style, staff, skills and shared values are the main interacting elements.

Peters and Waterman used the 7-S Framework to evaluate how success was achieved in some of America's best-run companies. They summarised these results in their influential *In Search of Excellence*, published in 1982, concluding that strategy rarely seemed to dictate a unique structural solution because other aspects of the 7-S Framework were also crucial influences. They distilled from their case studies some key ingredients of management excellence, such as remaining close to customers, fostering many leaders and innovators throughout the organisation, and treating all people in the economy as the root source of quality and productivity gains.

Seeking a Competitive Advantage

Many managers, academics and authors, in addition to those quoted, have propounded their own formulae for modern management success. From these, a number of themes have emerged that indicate the management 'Holy Grail' of competitive advantage is most likely to be found through a judicious blend of:

— *strategic planning and management*: the goals, plans and structures that provide the framework which influences, and is influenced by, other key factors;

— *management style*: the personality, behaviour and policies that characterise successful managers;

— *corporate culture*: the values, goals, rituals, and motivational forces that create a company's overall style;

— *people*: the development and availability of people with the skills, understanding, motivation, adaptability and attitudes needed;

— *systems and technology*: the relevant techniques and tools that help achieve planned objectives and open up new business opportunities.

Research at American management and research centres, like Harvard Business School and the Sloan School of Management at the Massachusetts Institute of Technology, have closely analysed how IT contributes to corporate success. Michael Porter of Harvard, for example, has written extensively about corporate strategies for competitive advantage. He has also developed techniques to identify the contribution made by IT to corporate success. Porter has defined what he calls the *value chain* as the basis for analysing how businesses operate as an overall system. The value chain is divided into *primary* and *support* activities. Primary tasks cover inbound logistics, operations, outbound logistics, marketing and sales, and service. Support cuts across primary activities, including aspects like human resource management, technology development and procurement.

According to Porter, advantages are often created through linkages between different activities in the value chain. This occurs where the cost or effectiveness of one activity, such as service, is affected by improvements in another activity, say operations. He has shown that IT is one of the most powerful tools for co-ordinating value chain activities and creating linkages between them.

LESSONS FOR INFORMATION MANAGEMENT

The background to management and organisation sciences in the previous sections is of more than just historical interest. The ideas and theories discussed have strongly influenced today's management and organisational approaches. They indicate that the following principles are important for successful information management:

Integrated corporate decision-making, planning, and direction. Information management must become an integral part of the processes which shape corporate goals, innovations, investments, deployment of resources and strategic plans. This means executives responsible for information management functions must understand the ideas and practices that contribute to corporate cultures and management styles. Equally, general management must be aware of the role that can be played by information management techniques like IT.

Broad-based IS design strategy. In order to meet real business needs successfully, the design of an information system must take account of its impact on issues like: relationships between the formal and informal organisation; the range of views that contribute to decision-making; job design and staff motivation; internal 'political' conflicts between different managers and departments; corporate standards and methods for justifying investments; the degree of autonomy allowed to different organisational groups and individuals; and other aspects of management style and corporate culture.

Effective information managers. The executives responsible for information management must be good managers in their corporate context. This requires skills in effective planning, staff motivation, and co-ordination with other managers and departments.

Co-operative IS partnerships throughout the organisation. Many people from various parts of an enterprise are likely to be affected by information management policies and IS developments: top executives, line managers, users at all management and staff levels, IS professionals, etc. All these different interests, backgrounds and skills need to be combined into effective partnerships, particularly for integrated systems that cut across many traditional organisational structures.

General management and organisational theories also provide valuable insights into the underlying beliefs and techniques that have influenced IS developments.

Taylorism and Computer Systems Design

Traditionally, as explained in Chapter 2, DP was generally seen as a 'management services' function reporting to the financial director. Other management services activities have been closely linked to scientific management techniques like OR and O&M. This placed DP squarely in the organisational camp that is most concerned with economic, technical and quantifiable aspects of defining and meeting business needs, rather than human and social factors.

The nature of computing technology also naturally attracts people with an interest in, and skills biased towards, logical problem-solving. To many IS experts, the design and development of an information system is often most interesting because of its technical challenges. Their notions of organisation and work design have been drawn largely from O&M methods, which in turn derived from Taylor's Work Study principles.

Frequently, as also discussed in Chapter 2, IS professionals may be remote from the daily realities of the applications for which they design computerised solutions. The barriers created by technical complexities and jargon, coupled with organisational remoteness, have often meant few users participated directly in designing the systems they were to use, other than through being interviewed by technical systems designers.

The result is that computer-based information systems have often been programmed with the implicit values, beliefs and practices of scientific management, although most systems designers and programmers may never have heard of Taylorism as such. Such software tends to focus primarily on formal organisation structures, which may bear little relation to actual, more informal work practices. This approach can be appropriate for applications that are intrinsically highly structured, routine and predictable, such as accounting and some transaction processing, modelling and simulation tasks. But, as computerised information systems have moved into the mainstream of most organisational activities, their Taylor-oriented, formalised designs could disrupt existing successful working methods based on other management principles.

Office Automation or Computer-aided Office Work?

Questions about the values and principles that underlie computer systems design came into prominence when IT began to move into ordinary offices. The term generally used to describe this development, *office automation*, implicitly assumes that the aim is to 'automate' work, in a similar way to manufacturing automation. In many organisations, the impact of computers on office work has indeed been to divide many jobs into discrete, specialised tasks, often under automatic control and performance monitoring — as had been recommended by Taylor in manufacturing factories. Most modern office work, however, has evolved from the Theory Y of human behaviour, with considerable attention given to job enrichment, individual motivation, group working, informal communications, autonomy and work flexibility. Using computers to impose Taylorism-type practices in such an environment can have detrimental effects.

For example, when word processing first became popular in the 1970s, specialist word processing and shared secretarial group pools were created. It was found later that this frequently caused a decrease in overall efficiency and a great deal of personal unhappiness. Jobs using word processors were often much less varied than those of other secretarial and typing work, which caused a rise in stress, boredom and error-proneness. This caused many secretaries and typists to be isolated from the executives and professionals they worked for and so lost a lot of their commitment to, and understanding of, the work they were handling. Managers and professionals then had to spend more time on relatively unproductive tasks, like photocopying, because they had lost valuable secretarial support.

Socio-technical design techniques provide an important alternative approach, which emphasises the use of computers to assist the performance of office work in ways most suited to the people and groups using them. Pioneering work in this form of *computer-assisted office work* was undertaken in Scandinavia in the 1970s, often prompted by requests from trade unions. Elsewhere, many other socio-technical applications and research projects have been successfully carried out. For example, Enid Mumford at the Manchester Business School in the

UK, has developed a technique of *participative systems design* for office information systems based on socio-technical principles. This involves users directly in helping to carry out systems design and analysis tasks. It aims to increase job satisfaction as a specific systems design objective and places emphasis on good organisation and work designs, as well as good technical designs.

A Balanced Approach to Systems Design

Computers have often been perceived as machines with a logic of their own that produce patterns of automation determined primarily by their technical capabilities. Michel Crozier, however, has pointed out that:

> "The computer does not provide, as was initially assumed, a single best technical or organisational solution. At first, computers provoked dreams (or nightmares) of a Taylorian paradise (or hell). In practice, computers have exploded the Taylorian myth that there was a particular optimum, scientific method of organising work around machines. They can handle a wide variety of different organisational forms, from extreme Taylorism to participative socio-technical designs."

Effective management control over computer-based information systems can be exercised only by recognising that technical systems design is a prime influence on organisation, job and task designs. Corporate and information management policies must, therefore, require that IS designers take explicit account of *all* aspects of the structures and working methods they are creating.

The remainder of this book explores the ingredients of an information management strategy that will produce the required balanced approach to IS activities, including systems design.

SUMMARY: THE MANAGEMENT CONNECTION

This chapter is a crucial part of the book because it provides a bridge between general management theories and specific information management requirements. It has shown that computer-based information systems are intrinsically bound up with corporate strategy structures, style and other management policies. An awareness of this broader management context is vital to the design of information systems that meet business, user, economic and technical goals. The natural orientation towards scientific management methods by technical IS professionals means that special care must be taken to ensure human and social aspects are given due attention, where appropriate.

PART 2

Developing an Information Management Strategy

4 The Information Management Strategy

STEERING INTO THE UNKNOWN

Part 1 (Chapters 1 to 3) has shown the extent to which computer-based information systems affect a huge variety of organisational activities. This may involve the introduction of innovations in:

— *organisational structures* to cope with the new services, products and working methods opened up by the technology;

— *management roles* within these new structures;

— *decision-making processes* using information systems;

— *services and products* offered to customers and clients;

— *working methods;*

— *job responsibilities;*

— *task skills;*

— *information management* systems and technology.

These changes can reverberate throughout an organisation. They create new opportunities, but also new uncertainties. They can enhance the standing of some individuals and departments — but reduce the influence of others. Long-standing working relationships and career expectations may be disrupted. Some people will gain more satisfying and better-paid jobs — others will have their jobs downgraded or eliminated. Corporate cultures and political power balances within them may be greatly altered.

The only certainty in this environment is that the future will be substantially different from the past. Steering a successful course into such unknown territory depends on having a clear sense of direction and the ability to respond effectively to unforeseen pitfalls and opportunities. That is why a corporate strategy for information management is *vital*.

This strategy must be comprehensive, without being cumbersome; set precise targets, while remaining flexible; steer a consistent long-term course, but be capable of making adjustments in the light of experience. It must be a strategy that gives as much consideration to managing changes *of* an organisation as to changes *within it*.

STEERING INFORMATION MANAGEMENT

There is no single formula for information management success that can be applied universally. The particular circumstances, applying at a particular time to a particular IS system, using particular IT capabilities, will be unique for each organisation, division, department or other group. The advice in this book, therefore, seeks to illuminate and define basic principles that can be incorporated into different strategies, plans and tactics appropriate to each circumstance. The following sections provide an overview of key imperatives that should underpin information management policies.

Ask 'Why?' Before 'When?'

There are many pressures on management to proceed as quickly as possible with IT investments. Growing awareness of the value of information systems to business success, plus rapid technical innovation, can stimulate a fear of 'being left behind in the information revolution'. The need to cut costs or 'keep up with' competitors can cause a sense of urgency in implementing IS plans and installing IT capabilities. These pressures should be resisted until an adequate analysis has been made of the reasons why an information management initiative may be needed. Time spent in the initial phases of diagnosing what is needed and how it can be achieved will pay handsome dividends by creating systems that meet genuine needs over a long period.

The willingness to think through requirements before acting is one of the hallmarks of the approach that has led to Japanese industrial and economic success. Japanese government departments and companies took stock of market needs, future technical trends and available national resources *before* developing their national and corporate strategies for the electronics industry and other activities. In a similar way, IS developments should be preceded by an investigation of market and organisational needs, business and technical trends, and the nature of existing systems and resources. Such a diagnosis should be wide-ranging, imaginative and focused on business and user needs. This process may use the stimulus of IT innovations to rethink broad traditional approaches. It can give an opportunity to look at what an organisation, or unit within it, is doing now and where it should be going in the future. Many improvements that flow from it may relate to policies and actions not directly concerned with introducing or developing new technology.

Information systems often fail because there have been hasty and inadequate analyses of what has to be done. This generally results in the implementation of systems designed primarily to fulfil short-term needs. Without an in-depth understanding of how these narrow aims fit into a more general perspective, much effort can be directed towards relatively unimportant tasks, or down the wrong track altogether. Frequently, poor diagnoses lead to the implementation of computer systems with insufficient capacity or flexibility to meet changing user demands.

Plan Long, Act Short

Strategies are concerned with long-term plans. This is necessary to ensure that today's investments continue to provide good returns for a long period — and do not become a strait-jacket inhibiting subsequent developments. There is a danger, however, that too much emphasis on strategic issues can miss more immediate opportunities. The rapid rate of IT innovation can also provide a spurious rationale for inertia, which runs something like this: "Any system we install today is likely to become outdated soon by quicker, cheaper and more powerful systems. So, wouldn't it be better to wait a little until something more cost-effective comes onto the market?"

However, such delays can lose the substantial benefits that could have accrued if the system had been installed earlier. Important practical experience will also be delayed, which postpones benefits gained when users move up the learning curve. These losses can more than outweigh the gains in price and performance obtained by waiting for a newer system. The need to think about and develop long-term plans should never become an excuse for prevarication. Prompt and sensible actions must form an integral part of IS plans, within a strategic framework that plans to build on investments over a long period.

Management Leadership

Top management involvement in, and backing for, information management policies is crucial. Without it, the best laid plans will fall apart in practice.

Information management cuts across many different management responsibilities and organisational structures. It can be a powerful weapon in internal management power struggles. As a potential threat to some managers' status and scope of responsibility, information management can also be a target for management opposition, conducted via direct or covert attacks. Top management must, therefore, not only give a clear direction to information management; it must also be seen to support the executives responsible for information management activities through practical acknowledgements of their status and authority. That commitment must be maintained visibly and be consistently refreshed and reinforced.

The most effective way of doing this is to make information management a senior corporate responsibility. The whole top management team should be seen to be continually questioning managers, staff, customers and others about the effectiveness of information systems. This will demonstrate the value they place on information management, as well as keeping them in touch with how systems are performing.

Top management should take a positive attitude to computer-based information systems in general, but be critical when examining specific proposals. Managers who are technological enthusiasts can be as damaging as those who are uninterested in IT. A balance must be struck between corporate needs and the momentum generated by IT innovation. In some cases, negative attitudes to computers have to be overcome at many levels in the company. Distrust of computers may be based on bad experiences with them in the past or may arise from anxieties about their impact on traditional ways of working. Such attitudes cannot be overcome by edict. A sensitive strategy is needed to understand the causes of existing perceptions and build new attitudes.

Top management leadership sets an example to others. When backed by appropriate organisational structures and educational support, it lays the foundation for the development and implementation of effective information management policies.

The Evolutionary Planning Cycle

Management and planning activities are often depicted as a linear process, beginning with the setting of objectives and ending with the implementation of the desired solution. In practice, many operations follow a more complex evolutionary cycle, without a clear-cut start and finish.

Adaptability to changing requirements and lessons learnt from experience is an important feature of the strategies and plans needed to create and implement information management policies. Figure 4.1 shows the main functions that must be performed to steer information management innovations. Even though it simplifies the process, the figure illustrates the variety of interactions that can take place between activities.

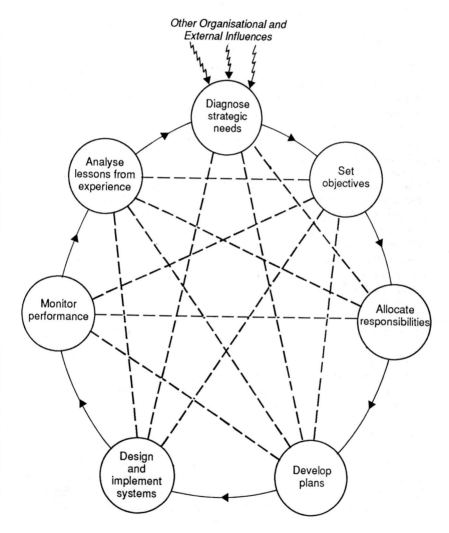

Figure 4.1   Key Elements and Interactions in the Information Management Process

Logically, the cycle starts with diagnosing why change is needed. Moving clockwise, this leads naturally to the setting of objectives. In order to achieve them, information management responsibilities throughout the organisation must be defined and allocated. Those responsible then develop detailed plans for designing and implementing systems. Actual experiences should be monitored and analysed in order to provide feedback into the diagnosis phase.

The reality is frequently very different. Only when forming a new company or embarking on a completely new development is it possible to start with a period spent purely diagnosing requirements. More typically, existing operations and systems are the starting point, with new ideas and aims bubbling up over time. The initial task is often to re-orient and adapt current policies and methods. A smooth clockwise progression around the activities shown in Figure 4.1 is unlikely to occur on most IS developments. The dotted lines in the figure describe just a few of the many other pathways through which elements interact directly. There are also external influences that can affect the strategy, such as competitive pressures, the national economic climate, government policies or a takeover by another company. The overall process is similar to the organic growth of biological organisms.

This has some important implications for the development of information management strategies. It is the reason why adaptability is such an important requirement. The whole process must be continuously nourished and reinvigorated to avoid stagnation. Top management must maintain an active involvement throughout the process, rather than just relying on giving an initial kick-start.

Unlike biological organisms, however, information management cannot rely on genetic inheritance to guide it to success. Systematic plans are needed to control developments; otherwise they may grow chaotically. Systematic, phased plans, with defined milestones and review procedures, must be established as the basis for guiding developments to meet the desired goals.

Encouraging Enterprise

Any major strategic innovation, such as a significant new information management initiative, involves a degree of risk-taking, particularly if substantial benefits are to be obtained. This demands an entrepreneurial approach, where management vision and instinct are encouraged, provided planned steps are taken to control progress so that the risks are minimised and the impact of any failures is contained. It does not mean that relatively conservative organisations must suddenly become a hive of entrepreneurial activity, but indicates that successful IS developments are often based on a management 'act of faith', as well as more analytical judgements.

Appropriate cost-benefit analyses must be carried out at some stage, as discussed in Chapter 8. However, over-exhaustive analyses can waste time and resources that could have been deployed on making actual progress. Excessive attention to detailed, quantifiable costs and benefits, can also divert attention from more imaginative and substantial advantages, which are often difficult to define precisely. Cost-benefit analyses should be complementary to the directional drive established through the intuition and knowhow of management, professionals and staff. This 'vision' can help to create greater commitment to a system than objectives which emerge from an anonymous and lengthy analysis.

As many information management projects involve a substantial element of risk, important unforeseeable outcomes are likely to occur. Some of these will bring unexpected benefits; others may be regarded as being failures and mistakes. Most users also tend to go through a tentative phase when systems are first introduced, while their skills and confidence increase and their anxieties are allayed. Such patterns of progress should be anticipated. Everyone involved should feel free to discuss their positive and negative experiences, without having to worry that they will be 'blamed' unjustly. Many information systems fail because they operate in a climate of fear. Some managers and users may even be led to believe that IT is such a miraculous force that any failures in its use are caused by personal inadequacies, rather than problems with the design or operation of the technology.

Systematic mechanisms need to be set up to ensure feedback from all levels of users (including that from customers, clients and other organisations) is monitored, analysed and acted on. Effective learning from experience, within a phased strategy, allows enterprise to flourish while ensuring risks are effectively controlled.

Partnership and Commitment

Many people may be involved in an IS project, such as:

— *senior corporate managers* responsible for controlling strategic developments;

— *line managers* directly responsible for the business area most affected by the system;

— *IS professionals* responsible for developing, implementing and running the technical system;

— *users* of the system;

— *education and training specialists* who need to upgrade skills and awareness;

— *personnel experts* responsible for managing the human transition to a new system, say in terms of new job conditions or salary scales;

— *customer service and public relations management and staff* responsible for handling any impact the system may have outside the organisation.

If a project is to be successful, everyone with an interest in it must work in unison to achieve common goals. Effective partnerships must be forged, particularly among those most directly concerned: managers, users and IS professionals. Otherwise, there is a danger that management responsibility could be split between corporate, line and IS managers, without anyone being in real control.

Clear definitions of responsibilities help to blend the right partnership. Business success should be the responsibility of business managers. IS professionals should take charge of the technical aspects of meeting business needs; they should also be respected by other managers as informed advisors and consultants who have valuable contributions to make to business decisions. Corporate managers need to ensure developments fit the strategic plan and general directives they set. All those involved should feel a commitment to the project's success by being given a tangible stake in influencing its course. For example, users can be directly involved in developments from an early stage by the provision of user-oriented applications development tools and business-trained IS professionals who work closely with user departments. Views should be actively solicited from anyone with a stake in the system and they should be given a tangible response to show their ideas have been considered, even if they have not been wholly accepted.

Such widespread participation could become unwieldy unless it is managed efficiently and with sensitivity to the various needs of different groups and individuals. Again, it is a question of incorporating controls and procedures within systematic plans. *Consultation* should not mean an abrogation of responsibility by those in charge of setting and meeting project targets. It is an important means of gathering information on practical user requirements, as well as encouraging commitment to the project, so should be regarded as an important and integral element in IS developments.

Supporting the Strategy

Establishing a strategy is insufficient in itself. It needs to be supported by continuing commitment to its implementation and evolution. Education and training plays a key role in supporting the strategy. Senior management must be educated to understand the principles, goals and practices of strategic planning. Everyone in the organisation must also receive appropriate levels of education and training in information management concepts and techniques relevant to their areas of responsibility, and IS specialists need to grasp modern business methods.

The impacts on organisational structures and job definitions made by an information system could require extensive changes to personnel policies, such as job grading, salary structures, recruitment and career development. The shortage of skilled IS staff may be a key constraint on fulfilling plans. Flexible and imaginative personnel strategies, combined with effective education and training initiatives, can contribute significantly to resolving many skills requirements. Education and training support for the IS strategy is discussed in more detail in Chapter 5. IS specialist staffing is examined in Chapter 6.

The Human and Organisational Context

Information systems have a value only in relation to the working environment in which they function. Enthusiasts may get excited by particularly clever, imaginative and versatile IT facilities, but from a business or public service perspective, such technical wizardry can be afforded only if it delivers tangible benefits. IT capabilities must, therefore, always be viewed in the context of the organisational system, corporate culture and human behaviour which determine its effectiveness. For this reason, the various traditions and techniques that have been developed to cope with organisational design, management control, job satisfaction, work efficiency and personnel motivation are examined in Chapter 3.

SUMMARY: THE MANAGEMENT OF CHANGE

This chapter has explained why the development of information management strategies and plans is concerned with the management of organisational change, not just technological innovation. It has emphasised some key characteristics of successful corporate approaches to information management:

Think before acting. Diagnose why changes are needed; analyse how they should be managed; and plan for them to be implemented in phased stages.

• *Plan for tomorrow, act for today.* Spend time preparing long-term strategies, to steer information management along appropriate routes; but act promptly to introduce appropriate systems so that benefits can be garnered and experience gained as quickly as possible.

Lead from the top. Senior management must give positive, but critical, support to IS initiatives and ensure information management has the required levels of authority and resources. This support must be expressed through highly visible policies and actions which are consistently sustained.

• *Evolve through adaptable, phased strategies and plans.* Information management is an open, evolving process with many complex interactions which are most effectively managed by systematic co-ordination that allows adaptations to be made smoothly, in a controlled way.

Be prepared for the unexpected. IS innovation involves significant uncertainties and learning experiences. An atmosphere should, therefore, be created where experiences are discussed openly, backed by objective performance evaluations, so that any mistakes can be rectified quickly and successes built on efficiently.

Create all-round partnerships and commitment. Everyone involved in IS developments should work harmoniously together and feel they have an individual stake in the system's success.

Ensure adequate education and training support is provided. A co-ordinated programme of education and training activities must be established to offer everyone opportunities to learn appropriate levels of information management and business skills and understanding.

Give high priority to organisational and human needs. Understanding the way organisations behave, how people are motivated and how effective management decisions are made and implemented is essential to understanding how information systems should behave.

5 The Role of the Information Manager

DEFINING RESPONSIBILITIES

The corporate information management strategy discussed in Chapter 4 should define the role, status, authority, areas of responsibility and general aims of information management functions. Without such a clear strategy and demarcation of responsibilities, information management will become a confused battleground.

The strategy should clarify *who* is responsible for *what* in IS developments. There will obviously be a need to manage special IS and IT resources. The role of information management at a corporate level and in intra-organisational activities is more difficult to define precisely. Relevant lines of communication and management reporting structures must, therefore, be specified unambiguously, after reaching agreements with those affected.

ESTABLISHING CORPORATE PRIORITIES

The corporate priorities underpinning the information management strategy should be stated succinctly and forcefully by the organisation's chief executive and its management board. These can be encapsulated in statements such as:

Information management is a key corporate strategic issue.

Information systems are key strategic resources.

Information management must be a top management responsibility.

Senior executives responsible for information management functions must have authority throughout the organisation to act as facilitators in ensuring maximum business benefits are obtained from IS investments.

The position of information management executives and functions within the corporate structure flow naturally from these principles.

The most significant task is to make the senior executive responsible for information management a full member of the top corporate management team. This team is responsible for activities such as finance, marketing, production, personnel, sales, etc.

The composition of the top management team varies between organisations. In some cases, it is equivalent to the board of directors. In others, there may be an executive committee of senior managers beneath a small, generally non-executive board. The chief executive officer, managing director or chairman may be the entrepreneurial or autocratic leader directing the work of the top management group; or there may be a broader sharing of decision-making among the team.

It is vital to establish information management at the same level as the other key corporate activities. In middle to large organisations, the information management job is so demanding that it should be the full-time job of a skilled manager. In smaller organisations, the executive responsible for information management, who could be the chief executive, may also have other responsibilities.

The person with top information management responsibility has been given a variety of titles, such as information manager or chief information officer. In some organisations, it has been the IS, information processing or MIS director who has been given the overall information management role. This book uses the term *information manager* to describe this role; the IS, Information Processing or MIS manager is taken to be the next level down, in charge of detailed IS planning and implementation. However, the title is unimportant in itself. It frequently relates to past job functions and particular organisational cultures. What is more significant is the scope, status and content of the role — and the ability of the information manager to make a productive contribution to corporate decision processes.

The information manager must establish an appropriate IS infrastructure and co-ordinate all IT resources. Many IS resources will be the direct responsibility of the departments, groups and individuals who use them. Frequently, users will take the prime initiative for, and control of, IS projects. From a strategic perspective, the main information management responsibility is to ensure that users achieve maximum benefits for themselves *and* the organisation as a whole.

The IS infrastructure will include technical standards, communications networks, corporate databases, data centres, IS specialists and other aspects which are examined later in this book.

FACILITATING SUCCESSFUL APPLICATIONS

The information manager must optimise the contribution of information systems to all areas of the organisation. This involves liaising with many managers, departments, groups and individuals. Overall, the aim is to be a *facilitator*: encouraging, supporting and advising users to make the most of IS opportunities. Frequently, information management and IS functions fail because they are perceived either as a rigid, centralised barrier to local initiatives and/or as technical enclaves with little to offer business activities. Information managers must seek to overcome these attitudes by showing they can provide support services that positively assist the rest of the organisation. For example, IS systems that act as:

— a *strategic enabler* helping to meet long-term aims and opening up new strategic options;

— a *management aid* to help executives carry out their responsibilities for business performance and creating appropriate organisational and working environments in their own spheres of influence;

— an *operational tool* to carry out particular tasks, at all levels in the organisation, and in most functions.

In liaising with the rest of the organisation, information managers and IS professionals should act as advisors, consultants and partners, not bureaucratic and jargon-shrouded technocrats. In addition to direct technical assistance in developing and running systems, they could provide:

— seminars, training courses and publications to educate general managers and staff in potential business opportunities opened up by IT;

— informal discussions and support to help formulate users' IS project aims before formal requirements analysis begins;

— close detailed liaison with users once systems are operational, for example through information centres and help desks (see Chapter 12);

— systematic elicitation and analysis of users' perceptions of the IS service and how it can be improved;

— advice and information on the likely impact of IS developments on organisational structures, the quality of the working environment, work practices and other management issues discussed in Chapter 3.

Many of the most successful IS projects have been championed by an influential user who understood the applications and was then 'sponsored' by a senior manager who gave it authoritative backing. Information management specialists should pay particular attention to identifying and supporting such user *champions* and project *sponsors*. Of course, if the champion is a manager of sufficient status in the organisation, he or she could also be the sponsor.

The intra-organisational liaison role of information management is a difficult one to perform successfully. It demands a good understanding of the organisational culture and business requirements, which involves a far broader range of management skills than the technically-oriented responsibilities of the traditional DP manager in the 1970s.

HANDLING EXTERNAL IMPACTS

Information management policies are increasingly having a direct effect on marketing, sales, customer services, product design, public relations and other operations focused outside the organisation. With the growing number of IS links to customers, clients, suppliers, retail agents, banks, etc, any problems with a computer-based system can have a detrimental impact on vital external groups and organisations. For example, if there is inadequate computing capacity in a network linking agents to corporate databases, the resultant delays and failures could cause agents to switch to a supplier with a better information system.

The friendliness and efficiency of an IS facility used directly by customers, such as ATM machines, can strongly influence attitudes to the whole company. In some applications, any interruption to an information service can be extremely costly or dangerous, for example, in financial services or air traffic control networks. Information managers should, therefore, be closely involved in formulating strategies and plans that support activities which go beyond the organisation itself.

Public Relations

Information management can have a direct impact on the image of the organisation, as well as specific products and services. Its *Public Relations* (*PR*) effects should, therefore, be included as an important element in the strategy.

For many years, computing itself suffered from a bad PR image both within and outside organisations. Some of this derived from fear of a strange new technology. There have also been many cases when a new system caused a deterioration in the quality of operations. Frequently, there has been a tendency to 'blame the computer' for human and organisational failings.

By considering its PR potential in a planned way, an information system can become a positive means of enhancing the image of a company or service. A thorough analysis of possible negative PR impacts can also help to improve the quality of the service offered. For example, the more 'user friendly' a system is when operated by the general public, the more likely it is that it will have a good PR effect. The provision of attractive brochures, leaflets, adverts and other PR aids can help to promote the advantages of a new system and forestall possible queries and complaints. Information managers should participate in planning PR activities for particular applications, or the organisation as a whole. The effective promotion of new developments can also help to attract IS professionals, which can be important when skilled staff are in short supply.

Regulations and Legislation

Many national and international regulations and laws can have significant implications for information systems. These include:

— laws on the protection of data privacy;

— copyright legislation;

— national taxation and pension regulations;

— telecommunications policy;

— health and safety rules (for example, covering the use of screen-based workstations);

— international rules governing the flow of data across borders;

— liability laws;

— Customs and Excise procedures.

Information management requirements for responding to such changes should be considered from the earliest stages, with IS specialists being involved in investigating likely costs and timescales for making necessary modifications to systems. Information managers should also try to maintain an early-warning system to detect forthcoming changes by encouraging IS professionals to participate in relevant industry, standards, and government bodies studying the issues.

The running of international networks can involve having to deal with a wide range of legislative regimes with different impacts on: the systems that can be used, information held, and data transmitted. For example, health and safety regulations in one country may prevent the connection of workstations used elsewhere. Wide variations in the rules governing the contents, access to and transmission of, database information can result from national data protection laws. (Chapter 12 discusses data protection and other legislation in more detail.)

BUSINESS ALLIANCES, TAKEOVERS AND MERGERS

IS links to external organisations and individuals are a vital strategic development for many organisations. The management of such linkages plays an important role in inter-organisational negotiations. For example, if there are plans to form a business alliance between a number of companies for a specific purpose, the ability to inter-link their IS capabilities may be essential. Overcoming IS incompatibilities can have a major impact on the schedules for creating business alliances and may even affect the overall viability of the plan. An existing IS infrastructure can also impose constraints on a company's plans for takeovers and mergers. Problems in combining computing and telecommunications capabilities can cause delays in progress, or the complete abandonment of the idea, even when it makes good business sense.

In developing an information strategy, therefore, one of the goals should be to maintain maximum corporate flexibility in case new alliances, takeovers or mergers are desirable. Adherence to international and industry standards, plus the allocation of high priority to the maintenance of system flexibility, are key methods of achieving these goals.

These considerations provide further strong support for the need to make information managers part of the top management team. The information manager must be involved closely in discussions and decision-making concerning any major corporate move, like business alliances or takeovers.

MANAGING IS EDUCATION AND TRAINING

A major responsibility of the information manager is to help co-ordinate the extensive education and training programmes needed to support IS strategies and developments. These range from general awareness courses to detailed training on specific information systems and products. It requires substantial investment in the provision of appropriate educational resources and in making time available for the people who are to be trained.

Education helps individuals to fulfil their own roles successfully and to participate effectively in working with others to satisfy corporate goals. For example, users should acquire the basic IT skills and knowhow necessary to carry out their jobs. They should also gain broader insights into the potential and limitations of the technology to enable them to contribute positively to developments and new application ideas. IS professionals, on the other hand, must keep their technical skills updated, which is difficult with such a rapidly-moving technology. They should also be encouraged, through systematic educational programmes, to learn about the organisation's business management techniques and users' practical working experiences and needs. This helps IS professionals to extend their involvement in general decision-making processes, opens new career paths for them, breaks down barriers that may exist with the rest of the organisation — and helps them to develop and run systems suited to real business conditions.

Formal in-house and external courses should be only part of the information management education and training plan. Many other techniques also have a valid role to play, such as:

— *workshops* to review and discuss topics in depth;

— *seminars and presentations,* which may be set up relatively quickly and informally, to pass on information and examine specific issues as they arise;

— *visits to other organisations* to learn about their experiences with similar information systems;

— *external conferences and seminars* on general subjects of relevance to immediate or future developments;

— *talks* by consultants and well known 'gurus';

— *systems suppliers' services*, including demonstrations, courses, seminars, books and brochures;

— *ad hoc day-to-day contacts* that can be an effective means of exchanging information and passing on expertise, so regular informal and social contacts between IS and other groups should be encouraged;

— *publications*, including reports on workshops and seminars, training manuals, introductory books, instructional texts and videos;

— *television and radio programmes*;

— *computer aided training*, such as CAI software and interactive video;

— *inbuilt software and online aids*, such as 'help screens' that are called up when the user is in doubt about what to do next.

These activities add up to a considerable amount of resources. Finding the time to do them is often extremely difficult given the usual business pressures on managers and staff. Costs, of course, should always be kept under tight control. Education and training programmes must, therefore, be efficiently co-ordinated to ensure resources are invested productively. Co-ordination is likely to be needed across the organisation as most people require some form of information management awareness and skills.

SKILLS OF THE INFORMATION MANAGER

The information manager and other IS executives need to combine three key skills to carry out their responsibilities effectively;

— general management ability;

— good understanding of corporate activities and the way the organisation operates;

— good technical expertise in developing and running information systems.

In practice, there is often an imbalance in these skills. It has been a common complaint, for example, that executives responsible for IS functions are more interested in technical wizardry than managing people and understanding the business. Putting general managers in charge of information systems to overcome this technical bias frequently fails because the manager has inadequate technical skills. This can allow IS developments to veer out of effective control or the manager to be 'captured' by the technologists and become an uncritical advocate of innovation for its own sake.

IS executives should be able to gain the respect of their colleagues both for their particular area of speciality *and* for their ability to participate in strategic planning. As information management crosses so many organisational boundaries, executives in charge must be particularly skilled in working co-operatively with other parts of the organisation.

The skills required of the information manager and senior IS executives are complex and demanding. There are likely to be few individuals with the full range of qualifications. Therefore, a comprehensive and relevant management training programme is the only way of ensuring that all information management aspects are managed successfully.

SUMMARY: TOWARDS THE IS STRATEGY

This chapter has examined the responsibilities of the information manager in the context of the strategy discussed in Chapter 4.

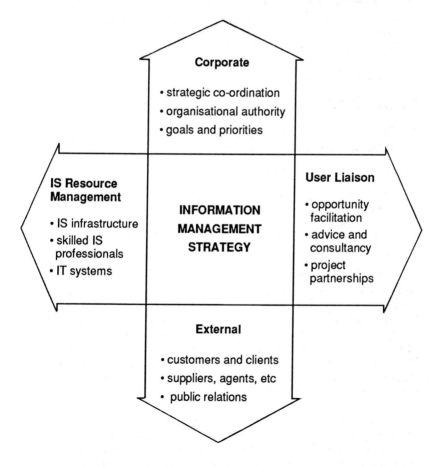

Figure 5.1   The Four Dimensions of an Information Management Strategy

Figure 5.1 summarises the four main dimensions of the information manager's role:

— *corporate* commitment to having the information manager as part of the top management team, participating in key strategic decision-making and co-ordination;

— *intra-organisational liaison* where the information manager and IS professionals act as facilitators and advisors to the rest of the organisation and help to manage activities that cut across organisational boundaries, such as IS education and training;

— *external relations* with outside organisations, users and others affected by IS developments and services;

— *IS resources management* of specialist IS and IT people, systems, and equipment.

Emphasis has been placed on the corporate and managerial aspects of the first three of these responsibilities. The skills and tasks involved in specialist IS resource management are the subjects of further chapters, starting with an investigation of IS and IT strategies in Chapter 6.

6 The IS Strategy

ORGANISING AND MANAGING THE IS FUNCTION

Within the strategic and management framework outlined in Chapters 4 and 5, plans must be established for organising and managing IS activities. This IS strategy should include the following main elements:

— *IS organisation*: where IS responsibilities fall within the corporate structure, particularly the role of any specialised IS functional units;

— *IS management*: how specialist IS personnel and resources are to be managed to meet business and user needs;

— *IT strategy*: the guidelines, standards and other procedures to be used to control IT hardware and software developments and operations.

The IT strategy must be seen as a subset of the overall IS plan. Technical aspects are important and must receive special attention. They must always, however, be kept within the context of the corporate and business goals to which they are being applied.

ARE IS DEPARTMENTS ESSENTIAL?

Before looking at how to manage the IS function, it is necessary to examine in what circumstances there is a need for such a specialist in-house group, or any IS experts at all.

The introduction of a new computer-based system, however small, needs assistance from people with IS expertise. Some of this expertise can be obtained by employing outside consultants and service companies. The system will be successful, however, only if people within the organisation have, or gain, sufficient understanding and skills to ensure the technical potential is applied effectively to business requirements.

Requirements of Smaller Organisations

At one time, virtually any computer system was so large and complex to operate that a special IS unit was obligatory. Now, many systems of substantial capability are easy to operate in ordinary office environments, but it would be a mistake for even the smallest company to use a computer without key executives and users receiving adequate IS training.

The less IS expertise available within a company, the more important it is to obtain independent advice early to ensure a suitable system is chosen. Many small organisations have been seriously damaged by obtaining apparently low-cost systems which prove to be totally inadequate and, ultimately, extremely expensive. The reliability, expandability and true ease of use of a system is particularly important to a small organisation that does not have the resources to buy itself out of the problems caused by having the wrong computer at the heart of its operations.

It may be reasonable for a small organisation to rely on outside expertise when selecting and introducing its first computer system. Over time, however, the organisation must build up its own expertise. The best way of doing this is by making information management and IS knowhow intrinsic to all corporate activities, as recommended in this book. Eventually, any organisation using IS capabilities should have its own IS expertise, if not its own specialist IS group. For smaller organisations, the best option is often to ensure that general managers and staff gain necessary IS skills. Employing just one or two IS specialists may cause problems because their career and salary ambitions are usually geared to those of the general IS profession, which may be difficult for a small organisation to meet.

When IS Experts Are Needed

At some point, even small computer systems may reach a stage where the technical needs become so important and complex that in-house IS specialists are essential. For medium and large organisations it is likely that such experts will always be necessary. However, the fact that some IS professionals are employed does not always imply that a separate IS group must be established. IT service companies offer a wide range of capabilities that can supplement in-house expertise and systems (see Chapter 9). Imaginative education and management strategies can also make effective use of non-IS specialists in 'technical' IS roles.

For example, some approaches to systems design bring users more directly into the systems analysis and design process (see Chapter 3). People who understand application and business needs can often be given the necessary technical skills to enable them to play a productive role in systems developments. Users can also produce software directly through applications development aids like 4GLs (see Chapter 2).

THE ROLE OF IS DEPARTMENTS

Chapter 5 explained why the information manager, or equivalent function, should be part of the top management team. The detailed management of IS services should be the responsibility of an executive (called the IS manager in this book) reporting directly to the overall information manager at board level.

The precise nature of the specialist IS units under the IS manager's control will vary considerably between organisations. In general terms, the IS manager could be considered as the equivalent of a DP manager, but with a much expanded corporate and technical remit. In some organisations there will be a large central IS division or department. In others, there may be a small central co-ordinating unit with the IS function distributed among operating divisions.

Whatever the strategy chosen, however, it is important to have clear corporate agreements on the role of specialist IS units and the allocation of responsibilities for IS developments and applications.

Centralised or Devolved IS Support?

One of the basic questions to be answered by the IS strategy is how the balance is to be maintained between corporate IS needs and the requirements of particular operating units, line managers and other groups and individuals. The key word is *balance*. It is wrong to think in terms of an 'either/or' decision about whether to opt for central or devolved control. When minicomputers, PCs and telecommunications first broke the dominance of centralised mainframes, there was much debate about whether this would mean the 'end of the DP department'. There were some attempts to go completely decentralised, but they frequently led to much wasted, unco-ordinated effort.

As explained in Chapter 6, the main aim must be to forge partnerships between IS professionals and the rest of the organisation. This means giving each partner responsibility for the things they do best with the ultimate decisions lying with those who have the relevant business responsibilities.

There are many reasons why an IS *centre of excellence* may be desirable:

Skills. One of the greatest constraints on IS is the availability of suitably skilled IS professionals. Their technical, remuneration, career and other needs cannot usually be satisfied outside a specialised IS unit.

Standards. The maintenance of technical standards is essential to enabling full corporate benefits to be gained from IS investments.

Cost control. Centralised co-ordination can achieve substantial economies of scale by being able to arrange deals with suppliers for the large-scale purchase of products and services. Having skilled and experienced staff to handle negotiations with suppliers, combined with effective standardisation controls, can also help to optimise the cost-effectiveness of investments.

Large-scale corporate IS resources. Many corporate applications, particularly those involving large amounts of data, are often most suited to big mainframe-type systems. Telecommunications systems, such as online TP applications, can consume substantial computing resources. These kinds of corporate workloads are often satisfied most efficiently through centralised data centres with sufficient IT capabilities and skills to cope with the demands of the applications.

Infrastructure co-ordination. An IS infrastructure that can evolve smoothly over a long period is the platform on which organisational success can be built efficiently and reliably. This can be done only by a unit with a broad perspective and high-quality skills.

Quality assurance. IS applications are so important to business operations that their quality and reliability cannot be left to chance. Disciplines must be introduced to maintain adherence to quality standards. Again, this can be achieved only by a unit with the necessary corporate authority and specialist skills.

Software expertise. Successful software developments depend on having highly skilled and experienced professionals to carry out work on major projects. User-based developments should be co-ordinated by these professionals to ensure that they meet corporate needs.

The centre of excellence which manages these types of corporate IS activities need not be a single division or department. Its nature will depend on particular IS and organisational requirements.

Organising IS Activities

Figure 6.1 illustrates the broad categories into which IS activities can be divided:

— *development* of the IS infrastructure and specific applications;

— *user support* in the development and operation of applications;

— *service management*, including the running of data centres;

— *network management*, development and operations, which overlap with the other categories.

In addition, there are two general functions that cover all activities:

— *administration*, such as secretarial, financial, accounting and library services, some of which may be drawn from other departments;

— *strategic control* through overall policies, guidelines and infrastructure plans.

IS development is the core of specialist IS activities. It includes tasks like systems design and analysis, programming, database design and technical feasibility studies.

User support is needed at all stages of the IS life cycle, from developing new applications to help-lines after systems have gone live. The skills required in support functions are oriented towards organisational requirements, such as business analysis and O&M. The support should also aim to help users understand and develop their own systems, through information centres, training and other facilities.

Data centres with powerful and complex systems must have specialist operations and support policies. Communications networks demand their own management focus because they bring together distinct telecommunications and computing technologies and approaches. The network function may draw much of its resources from other IS groups, like development and data centres, but must be an independent management function to ensure it gets appropriate attention. These IS activities are examined fully in Part 3 (Chapters 7 to 12).

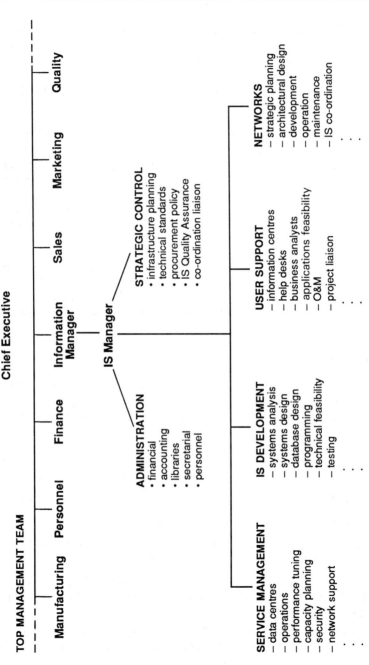

Figure 6.1   IS Organisational Structure

Figure 6.1 is intended to be a guideline to give a feel of the IS activities involved and the way in which they can be grouped. For simplicity, it is depicted as a single division or department. In practice, as has already been emphasised, organisations will have to work out the blend of centralised and decentralised management controls and organisational structures that are most suited to their own circumstances.

These IS structures could vary over time within the same organisation. For example, if IS is moving from a highly centralised mode of operation to one with greater user participation, it may be appropriate to put more emphasis on having a great deal of technical expertise within user support functions. As users become more experienced, some of this technical expertise could move back into development and other IS functions. The number and location of data centres could also vary over time.

For some projects, at particular stages of their development, it may be desirable to place technical staff directly under the control of business line managers. When the project matures and less technical effort is needed, the IS professionals could move to other projects, or into general IS functions.

RESPONSIBILITIES OF THE IS MANAGER

Given the rapidly changing technical and business environment in which IS must operate, structural flexibility is vital. At the same time, there must be central co-ordination to ensure all IS human and technical resources are used efficiently and effectively.

The IS manager will be responsible for a variety of activities, including:

— helping to formulate corporate information management strategy;

— establishing and managing the IS strategy;

— planning IS resource requirements: staff, software, hardware, telecommunications, accommodation, etc;

— working with managers in the rest of the organisation to identify how responsibilities are to be allocated for particular IS projects and applications developments;

— co-ordinating IS resources and services throughout the organisation, including the direct management and control of those within the IS function;

— promoting the work of the IS department to the rest of the organisation and externally, where appropriate.

The IS manager should have similar technical and business skills to the information manager, but with more emphasis on the ability to manage and run the detailed aspects of information systems.

Handling IS/User Partnerships

Managing any substantial IS development involves steering a variety of interacting business, technical, economic and human factors towards a common goal. This process is difficult enough in itself. When it also cuts across organisational boundaries, it could result in organisational tensions and infighting which make a successful outcome improbable, unless there is a well-planned approach to sharing responsibilities.

Before any kind of working partnership can be formed, the IS department and IS professionals must win the respect of the rest of the organisation. Some technically excellent IS departments lose users' confidence because they are unable to communicate in lay language, or are more concerned with improving technical innovation than satisfying real business needs. Technical incompetence, on the other hand, will undermine efforts to work closely with users in analysing and solving their practical requirements.

Plans should be prepared to promote the IS department to the rest of the organisation through newsletters, joint meetings, social integration of personnel and internal PR exercises. IS should be a familiar and welcomed part of everyday organisational practices.

Effective working partnerships will be easier to establish for specific projects if the overall organisational climate encourages positive attitudes to IS. Otherwise, valuable time has to be spent trying to overcome tensions and misunderstandings that are caused if there is a 'them' and 'us' attitude between IS professionals and users. Partnerships will be most effective if they are managed with structured, systematic techniques. Clear responsibilities should be defined, targets set and milestones monitored. This will avoid the partnerships drifting vaguely or going off-course because 'management by committee' leaves no-one in real charge. Figure 6.2 illustrates the likely composition of a project team. It is shown as a round table to indicate the importance of avoiding the creation of unnecessarily hierarchical and bureaucratic structures; the project should be seen as a team effort at all stages.

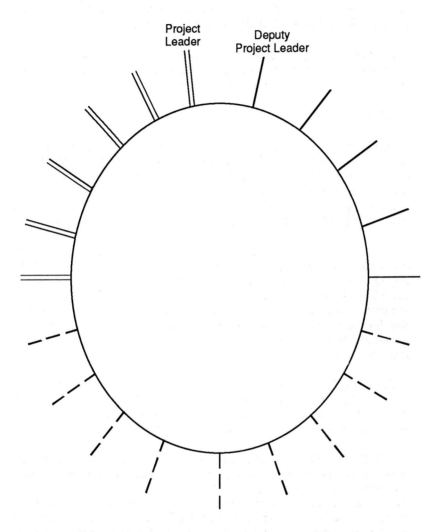

Project
Leader

Deputy
Project Leader

══════ Primary-user Representatives

────── IS Specialists

─ ─ ─ Representatives from secondary users and other relevant functions

Figure 6.2   Composition of a Project Team for IS Developments

The project leader should often be the senior executive from the system's primary users. The IS manager or other IS executive can play a valuable role as deputy project leader. The team could include other representatives from the primary user and IS functions, as well as from other groups affected and who can contribute positively to the work of the team. In addition, the use of specialist subgroups within the team enable many different tasks to be co-ordinated. For example, IS specialists could work in technical subgroups reporting to the senior IS executive on the team.

The most successful projects often include input at all stages from those affected at the grassroots, as well as from strategic and general management levels. For example, in office automation projects, secretarial staff can provide valuable help in ensuring systems meet real operational needs. Similarly, professionals and executives using decision-support systems must be consulted *as users*, not just in their formal organisational roles.

IS Resource Management

The bedrock of the IS manager's role is the provision of high quality, reliable and responsive IS services. Systems must be developed; standards set; equipment and software selected; applications run; plans established and fulfilled; technical IT innovations monitored; and a multitude of other tasks performed. IS managers must ensure sufficient numbers of IS professionals are available when needed to complete these tasks. Such people, however, are usually in short supply so much of an IS manager's time is likely to be taken up finding, controlling and motivating suitably skilled IS staff.

In many respects, the management of IS professionals should follow the same human relations and personnel policies that apply in other areas of the organisation. However, there are some special requirements that must be taken into account:

Manpower planning. The pattern of demand for IS skills will vary as systems evolve. During periods of innovation, there will be a high demand for development staff, people with skills in converting between systems and those capable of facilitating the introduction of new systems. At other times, the prime need may be to keep systems ticking over: providing efficient data-centre services, systems maintenance and user advice. Rapid IT innovation changes technical skills profiles. Plans must be developed to identify what these manpower requirements are likely to be, and how they should be met.

Recruitment. The shortage of staff can make recruitment an extremely expensive activity. The use of specialist recruitment agencies and costly advertisements in the press are often necessary because so many companies are fishing in the same small resource pool. Recruitment can be most cost-effective if a degree of flexibility is maintained in the type of experience being looked for, rather than limiting the search to the narrow range of skills needed at the time. In some cases, the skills gap can be met by looking for people within the organisation who can be retrained. These can either be professionals with other existing skills or general business staff who have the potential to understand the necessary IS techniques.

Training. Training policies should be closely integrated with manpower planning and recruitment. They should help IS professionals to be more flexible in moving between different types of systems and development methods. Training can also assist non-IS staff to carry out tasks like: business and systems analysis, applications development, and user support. Other aspects of education and training were discussed in Chapter 5.

Motivation. It is natural and desirable for IS professionals to be motivated by interesting technical challenges. Unfortunately, this is frequently associated with a disinterest in user aspects of systems. As a result, many IS professionals get bored when they are not involved in innovative technical developments. IS managers must take this into account in seeking to keep IS experts continuously motivated, say by becoming more involved directly with users and the success of the application.

Career development. A dual-track approach to careers for IS professionals should be offered: one path leading to mobility between IS jobs and the rest of the organisation, the other enabling some experts to pursue a purely technical track, with opportunities for promotion to status and salary levels equivalent to senior managers. Movement into IS from other parts of the organisation should also be encouraged, where appropriate.

Consultants and contract staff. The most effective solution to some IS manpower needs is to use outside consultancies and specialists on fixed contracts. *Contract staff*, for example, can help to satisfy peak demands, removing the need to employ permanent staff who may no longer be required when the major development effort is over. Contractors can also fill the gaps created by staff shortages, illness, holidays or other temporary factors. Highly experienced consultants can be employed to supplement in-house management and technical skills. Outside staff should always be fully integrated into overall IS management controls, with clear targets set for defining how performance on the contract is to be assessed. Potential friction between permanent and temporary staff, for example, over the higher salaries contractors may earn, should be dealt with sensitively. Consultancies and contract agencies should guarantee to provide a suitable replacement to the original appointment, should the need arise.

Remuneration and job grading. The shortage of skilled staff combined with their key value to vital business systems has enabled IS staff to demand, and get, job conditions that are superior to other equivalent groups. For example, IS professionals may get more money, at a younger age, and after a shorter time in the organisation than more established groups. Standard company job grading procedures have often been bypassed because they would produce job terms that would be unattractive to IS specialists. Personnel policies must take account of these special IS needs without causing dissatisfaction elsewhere in the organisation.

Many of the issues relating to IS professionals can be resolved satisfactorily only if they are supported by general management policies and attitudes in the organisation. And it is a further example of the importance of integrating the IS strategy with other corporate plans.

THE IT STRATEGY

The prime aim of the IT strategy is to provide a controlled technical framework that optimises corporate efficiency while giving as much freedom as possible to tailor each application to local needs. This involves setting standards and guidelines which:

— enable the organisation to use its combined strength and expertise in dealing with suppliers;

— make all systems as *open* as possible, so they can be adapted and inter-linked as required to match individual, group or corporate needs.

Technical Standards

As discussed in Chapter 1, major international standardisation efforts have been made to promote 'open systems'. The lack of such standardisation has been a major limiting factor in enabling systems to be integrated within, and between, organisations. It also causes costly, time-consuming and error-prone conversions when replacing outdated systems.

The aim of technical standardisation is to promote:

— efficient interworking between systems;

— portability of software and hardware between systems, applications and users;

— sharing of data, hardware and software between different parts of the organisation;

— effective systems development techniques;

— mobility of technical and user skills;

— smooth evolution as systems grow and adapt to meet changing circumstances;

— the widest possible choice of systems and equipment.

This involves the setting of standards in the following main activities:

— communications and network architectures, protocols and interfaces;

— operating systems that define what applications software can be used;

— hardware equipment and interfaces, covering mainframes, PCs, departmental minicomputers, workstations, terminals, data storage, printers, etc;

— system development approaches, such as software engineering methodologies and tools, programming languages and project management techniques;

— database management systems;

— user interfaces, including software interaction, screen design, documentation and physical ergonomics.

The standards chosen must relate to immediate and long-term practical needs. Consideration must be given to existing systems, not just what will be appropriate in five and ten years' time.

All corporate standards should take account of general IT standardisation trends internationally, nationally and within specific industries. Frequently, there are a number of potential standards vying for acceptance. Businesses usually cannot afford to wait for these conflicts to be resolved, so judgments must be made in choosing standards that are likely to remain of value, even if they are not subsequently universally accepted.

Users must avoid being over-optimistic about the degree of compatibility that follows from accepting an apparent standard. There are often many dialects, exceptions, additions and other variations which can cause incompatibilities between systems that theoretically meet a common standard. Increasing attention is, therefore, being given to backing standards with conformance tests. These help to define precisely what aspects of a standard are met, but may not say much about the performance and quality of the product tested.

Purchasing Policies

Technical standards help define the policies that are used to select systems and suppliers. If, for example, there is a decision to standardise on an operating system for certain types of systems (like PCs or departmental minicomputers), the hardware options are then limited to the equipment that runs that particular operating system.

In order to maintain flexibility, it is important to choose standards that offer a choice of potential suppliers, wherever possible. This has been made more feasible by the growing recognition by suppliers of the need to meet joint standards. The availability of plug-compatible hardware for popular systems also helps to ensure that standardisation and other corporate IT policies remain adaptable to various specific needs, rather than becoming a strait-jacket.

In some circumstances, the choice of a supplier or system will be dictated by existing investments or the nature of the application. It may not be worth the effort, for example, to convert from a non-standard operating system until the end of the natural life of the particular task it is supporting. Some applications may be best performed on a non-standard system from a specialist supplier.

Nevertheless, central co-ordination is needed to avoid such exceptions becoming the rule. A common way of helping to achieve this is through a *preferred suppliers* list covering hardware, software, maintenance, training, personnel agencies, consultancies and other services and products. By having preferred suppliers, the organisation can enter long-term agreements which obtain substantial cost and service advantages. It promotes adherence to standards and minimises waste and mistakes that can be made locally by inexperienced users when negotiating with suppliers.

The following are some of the criteria that may be applicable when choosing a preferred supplier:

— ability to provide support and service levels at all locations, including internationally if necessary;

— evidence of long-term financial viability;

— provision of a wide range of products and services which meet required standards;

— expertise and resources to address the range of applications in the organisation;

— sufficient research ability and financial resources to remain in the forefront of IT developments;

— plans to keep in the mainstream of industry developments, with a commitment to pertinent international or other broad standardisation efforts;

— proof of a good track record in keeping customers satisfied;

— specialist expertise where appropriate.

Controlling IS Investments and Budgets

The IT strategy is often resented because it is perceived primarily in terms of restrictive centralised constraints over local initiatives. This may arise because the 'strategy' consists of little more than the piecemeal imposition of standards and supplier controls, the reasons for which are poorly understood.

The IS or information manager may have the right to sign-off any IT investments above a certain amount, anywhere in the organisation, in an attempt to implement corporate policies. On its own, this is a crude method which is frequently bypassed, particularly as falling prices enable some systems to be obtained under other budgetary categories, like 'office equipment'.

In order to overcome such problems, and to control IS investments in an effective and equitable manner, the following actions should be intrinsic to IT strategy:

— develop the strategy, including specific budgetary controls and standards, in partnership with the rest of the organisation;

— explain the reasons for having central corporate standards, supplier policies and other central co-ordination, highlighting local as well as corporate benefits;

— regularly review and update standards and purchasing policies in the light of past experiences and current IT industry developments;

— allow users to have a say in how the IS department allocates resources under its direct control;

— avoid clumsy and bureaucratic control mechanisms which cannot allow for local variations, provided the need for breaking or bending standard procedures has been well argued.

SUMMARY: EFFECTIVE MANAGEMENT OF IS RESOURCES

This chapter has described the basic principles of how to develop and manage the IS strategy which turns information management goals into detailed systems and live applications. The following themes have been emphasised:

The broader context. The IS strategy will make business and organisational sense only if it is integrated into broader corporate decision-making processes.

A balance between corporate and local needs. There are strong arguments for centralised IS controls *and* for local user direction of IS applications. Therefore, a prime IS management task is to work out the optimum balance between these forces.

Partnerships between IS specialists and the rest of the organisation. One of the most serious traditional IS problems has been the organisational divisions and tensions that have existed between IS specialists and the rest of the organisation. These barriers must be broken down and genuine partnerships forged in order to establish an IS strategy that will be understood and respected by everyone involved.

The business pay-offs from standards. Technical standardisation is the backbone of an effective, efficient and flexible IS strategy. Business managers and users must appreciate how these standards help them to gain optimum advantage from their own systems, even if they cannot be expected to understand the technical complexities of detailed standards.

PART 3

Turning Plans into Successful Information Systems

7 Managing the IS Life Cycle

THE NEED FOR A PLANNED APPROACH

The successful creation and operation of information systems depends on having effective co-ordination of a large number of tasks, which may involve many business activities, technical facilities, people and suppliers. This control needs to continue over the whole lifetime of an application, which could be many years — even a decade and more.

A common cause of IS problems lies in the over-hasty rush into implementing systems before there has been an adequate analysis of what it is supposed to achieve. Frequently, an attempt is made to do everything in one push, rather than construction projects in well-defined stages that allow for adjustments to be made in response to practical experiences.

It is natural for managers to want to try to get business benefits as quickly as possible. Careful planning may seem to be a time-wasting luxury. Detailed diagnoses of what is wanted and the optimum way of proceeding may appear to frustrate the need to get immediate returns on investment. However, any short-term gains from such an ill-advised dash to IS innovation is likely to prove to be fool's gold.

Many organisations have found to their considerable cost that if they commit themselves prematurely to the wrong IS route, getting back on course wastes a considerable amount of valuable time and resources, and loses business as well as customer goodwill. The effort invested in establishing a structured IS management methodology will pay long-term dividends, as well as ensuring that real benefits are obtained at a sustainable speed.

Defining Aims and Means

In order to define appropriate targets and the means of achieving them, IS management must find suitable answers to some basic questions, such as:

Why have an information system The reasons for each new system or application must be carefully analysed and justified. Potential benefits and costs must be assessed imaginatively, but realistically.

What should the system do? Detailed requirement specifications must be established. Priority must be given to practical user support, such as appropriate system interfaces, understandable documentation, training, and ongoing advice backup. Requirements during the transition to a new system and long-term capabilities must also be taken into account.

Who should supply and develop IS facilities? Decisions must be made about who will supply various aspects of the system and related support: hardware and software vendors, consultants, in-house IS professionals, outside and internal trainers, specialist maintenance and recruitment companies, etc.

How can the objectives be achieved? A plan must be developed covering all aspects of developing and introducing a new system. Even where the system is being put together from 'off-the-peg' packaged products, or is being developed completely by an outside supplier, the detailed design, building, testing and implementation process must be charted in advance and continuously monitored durng the whole life cycle of a system or application.

The focal points for these questions, and their answers, are the organisational, business and human requirements which determine the results that must be delivered. Although complex technical solutions may be needed, management must insist that lucid and understandable explanations are provided to describe IS objectives, performance, benefits and problems.

THE IS LIFE CYCLE

A structured approach to IS management starts by identifying the main discrete phases in the life of a system. Each of these can then be broken down into simpler units containing a manageable number of tasks and activities, with well-defined objectives.

At an overview level, the key ingredients in the IS management life cycle are:

— *defining user requirements*: carrying out detailed feasibility studies and cost-benefit analyses to find out the requirements that must be fulfilled by the completed system;

— *creating operational specifications*: analysing user requirements and technical options to specify the characteristics of the IS functions that must be provided;

— *choosing suppliers*: finding who can best meet user and operational requirements;

— *developing systems*: the process of building systems to meet user and operational requirements, which may involve considerable work by in-house IS professionals;

— *introducing new systems*: preparing for and implementing the system when it is ready to be used;

— *providing the IS service*: running day-to-day operations;

— *adaptation*: monitoring performance, technical innovations and changing user needs to ensure the system evolves successfully.

In addition, all activities must be supported by:

— *quality controls* to establish and maintain appropriate standards throughout the life of a system;

— *education and training programmes* to provide necessary skills: special IS expertise to IS professionals; relevant IS understanding and operational knowhow to the rest of the organisation; and appropriate business knowledge to IS people.

This life cycle is summarised in Figure 7.1. It is shown as a circle to indicate it is not a linear process that ends with implementation. All the elements influence each other, in a similar way to the overall information management strategy summarised in Figure 4.1. For example, something learnt during developing or introducing a system can provide vital feedback to user and operational requirements, or experience gained in the day-to-day operational service can be directly affected by a new user requirement. The whole cycle is in a continuous state of evolution. For simplicity, however, all the possible interactions are not shown in Figure 7.1.

Engineering a Solution

Ideally, there should be a complementary range of techniques and tools covering all activities in the life cycle, from planning and analysing user requirements onwards. Such a total *information engineering* solution would eliminate inconsistencies and incompatibilities between different phases. This would cut down errors and make the whole process more reliable and flexible.

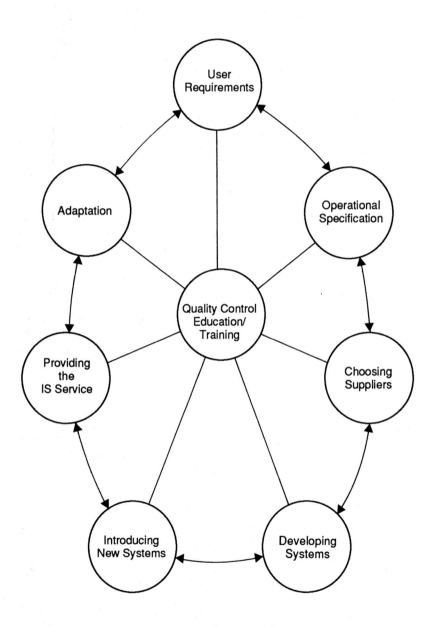

Figure 7.1   The IS Life Cycle

There have been many advances towards this ideal (discussed in more detail in Chapter 10). For example, structured systems analysis and design techniques are widely used, supported by a growing array of computer-aided software engineering tools; and the automatic generation of code from design specifications is helping to reduce the problems created in moving from specifications to coded programs.

However, even when there are accepted solutions to all activities they may be too expensive or demand too much of an upheaval for most users. Investments in existing techniques and tools cannot be suddenly abandoned. There are also many operational systems developed using unstructured methods which still have to be maintained, enhanced and integrated with the new developments.

The aim of a structured IS management plan should be to introduce effective information engineering methods wherever appropriate. This must be done within a strategy that gives high priority to establishing standards which promote overall consistency, but allow for evolutionary flexibility. It will then be possible to move smoothly and efficiently from the existing situation towards more advanced, integrated solutions.

The main phases of the life cycle are examined in subsequent chapters. Quality controls are the subject of the next section; and the need for education and training has been discussed throughout the book, particularly in Chapter 5.

QUALITY MANAGEMENT

The 'Quality Movement' has been a significant management trend in the 1980s, as mentioned in Chapter 3. Its aim of establishing effective *Quality Assurance (QA)* controls through a reliable *Quality Management System (QMS)* should also be applied to information systems.

An effective QMS must be based on:

— *defined quality standards*, including relevant methods, techniques and tools, for a common approach on different projects;

— *quality plans* specifying the quality levels that must be achieved at corporate, departmental, group, project, and individual levels;

— *continuous review and monitoring procedures* to ensure the QMS remains relevant despite changes in the technologies and methods employed.

QA should be a corporate function, with independent representation in the top management team. Such top management commitment is important to maintain the quality drive throughout the organisation. It is not much use, for example, to provide a high quality retail EPOS system if the quality of products and customer service in stores is poor. These QMS principles apply to any activity. IS developments have particular additional needs, and a distinct QA function should be identified for IS developments.

Controlling IS Quality

Many QA approaches originated in manufacturing industries, where it is relatively easy to ensure that products maintain a specified standard once the manufacturing process has been verified as meeting QA requirements. Regular production-line inspections can then adequately monitor continuing performance levels.

A *Software Quality Control* (*SQC*) system, however, must deal with a more complex development process and an intangible product. Software exists primarily as specifications, designs, program procedures and data structures. The software production process is relatively trivial, and the overall information system is usually difficult to pin down. User requirements are multifaceted and fluid. A wide range of hardware, software, data and communications may be involved, with facilities being continually altered, added and replaced.

SQC procedures can be effective only if structured systems engineering techniques are used throughout the IS life cycle, from business requirements analysis to detailed program coding. This kind of disciplined framework is needed to maintain consistency across all activities, at all times. QA procedures must therefore be implemented in all stages of the IS life cycle. The review and inspection of final systems and software products should check:

— conformance to standards;

— adherence to correct procedures;

— support by consistent documentation that can be traced through the life cycle.

These SQA checks cannot, in themselves, guarantee the quality of the content of the designs, program procedures and data models that have been created. The ultimate quality of the information system produced depends on the skills of those managing and carrying out the processes. QMS provides the foundations on which these skills can flourish.

The IS Quality Function

QA responsibilities should be independent of the group being evaluated. QA functions within IS activities should have a reporting line to the corporate QA director or a manager who is not also responsible for the system being approved. Without this independence, QA professionals could succumb to a variety of internal pressures to lower quality standards or bypass QMS procedures. Responsibility for the technical quality of the finished system should rest with the relevant project manager, but some IS knowhow is needed by the person co-ordinating QA on software developments. QA expertise gained in product manufacturing is an inadequate preparation for evaluating technical IS procedures and being able to talk meaningfully with systems analysts and programmers.

The quality plan should use the growing range of widely-agreed IS and QA standards wherever possible. For example, in NATO military systems, there are Allied Quality Assurance Publications (AQAPs) which can be used; AQAP-13 for instance is specifically about software. ISO 9001 from the International Standards Organisation can be used as the basis for a QMS in IS developments. QA standards used must be relevant to practical IS activities and should be continuously reviewed and updated. Instructions for their use must be clear and precise.

It must also be remembered that there is more to an information system than its technical development. The resultant service is usually an integral part of organisational activities, so QA controls are also needed for IT applications from a business and user perspective. The manager with corporate QA responsibility should ensure that there are co-ordinated, consistent QMSs in all areas of the enterprise.

SUMMARY: IS LIFE CYCLE OVERVIEW

As an introduction to the remainder of Part 3, this chapter has briefly summarised the key elements in the IS life cycle. It has emphasised the value of maintaining systematic, structured approaches through all phases of the cycle, supported by effective corporate policies for quality control and education and training. The scene has now been set for looking at the practicalities of IS systems developments.

8 Defining Applications Requirements

MORE THAN COMPUTER LOGIC

Computers are precise machines; organisations and people are not. There is a great deal of ambiguity and continuous variability in the way enterprises function, people interact, and work is performed. Therefore, information management must consider more than just those activities which are suited to being turned into the systematic models, automated procedures, and quantified data that characterise computer logic.

Some information management objectives are best achieved without computers; for example, by changing non-computerised procedures or improving staff motivation. Even when computers have a role to play, their predilection for programmable routines should not be allowed to dominate in all circumstances. More human-oriented approaches and IS facilities, including careful attention to user-system interactions, are also important.

The first phase of the life cycle involves investigating user requirements to identify the applications to be included in the IS plan. This is done primarily through feasibility studies and cost-benefit analyses. As a result, operational requirements can be drawn up, which become the basis for selecting and developing actual systems.

MANAGING THE FEASIBILITY STUDY

Feasibility studies must be steered by the kind of user/IS management partnership discussed in Chapter 6. Depending on its scale, the actual study could be carried out by a team of people, or by an individual. It must, however, be the responsibility of a senior business manager to decide whether or not the results make sound organisational and business sense.

Feasibility studies should investigate how computer-based information systems make an impact in four main areas:

107

Organisational: corporate structures; management responsibilities and chains of command; interactions between groups and individuals within the enterprise; internal and external communications; locations of offices, manufacturing plants and other facilities; regional and global responsibilities; innovations to existing products and services; creation of new products and services; and other overall business aspects;

Personal and social: job designs; working methods; personnel policies; human factors in systems and equipment design; staff consultation and industrial relations; skills requirements; training; motivation of managers and staff; and other issues concerning the quality of the working environment;

Economic: adding value; improving quality; enhancing productivity; saving costs; reducing staffing levels; returns on IS systems, people and equipment investments; and other likely benefits and costs;

Technical: procedures to be implemented; data to be managed; existing systems to be used and enhanced; new systems to be evaluated and introduced; in-house developments; conversions between old and new systems; and other detailed technical activities needed to select, design, implement and run the final system.

Technical aspects must be subservient to the others, but must be given appropriate weighting to ensure proposals remain feasible. The aim is to produce a balanced picture of desirable applications that can be achieved within acceptable budgetary and technical resources.

Setting Future Priorities

The feasibility study's short-term aim is to help decide whether or not to proceed with a project and to define the initial system outline. It also establishes the criteria on which the project's success will be judged throughout the system's life cycle. For example, if the study specifies that the prime aim is to cut the number of staff, subsequent effort will be focused largely on that aspect. This could mean insufficient attention is given to other opportunities, like using staff more creatively and productively.

IS developments need a strong business or user focus to give a clear sense of direction. Trying to aim at a disparate array of objectives can be confusing, even if each objective is valid in its own right. The feasibility study should, therefore, aim to undertake broadly based analyses to support a sharply focused vision, often derived from the instinctive belief of a senior manager or other application champion. Studies must be entered with an open mind and a willingness to investigate options objectively.

Potential applications could originate from the four areas listed previously (organisational, personal and social, economic and technical). There may be an organisational demand for a particular application; an individual or group may perceive an opportunity; the need for costs savings may be the chief imperative; and/or new technological capabilities may suggest potential IS or business innovations. Refining a diversity of possibilities, ideas, opportunities and problems into a cohesive plan is what the feasibility study must ultimately aim to achieve.

Terms of Reference for the Study

The feasibility study's terms of reference must provide precise guidelines, but be sufficiently flexible to allow for new factors to be taken into account as the study progresses. As many issues as possible should be anticipated, even if some may initially be defined as 'not applicable at present'. Many troublesome difficulties can arise at a later phase of the IS life cycle if something important has been forgotten during the feasibility study.

The following are some of the main factors that should be covered in the terms of reference:

— scope and limits of the study, including applications, activities, departments, proposals, etc, to be covered;

— managerial responsibilities;

— members of the study team, how responsibilities are allocated among them and who else must be consulted;

— interaction with other studies, projects, etc;

— any relevant IS policies, such as technical standards and preferred suppliers;

— budgetary constraints and resources available;

— general corporate or organisational requirements that must be considered, such as relationships with other departments and industrial relations procedures to be followed;

— any external factors that must be considered, for example government legislation or the activities of competitors;

— basic schedules and deadlines;

— milestones along the way to final completion, at which progress can be evaluated;

— general reporting mechanisms throughout the project, including report formats and the need for comprehensible management summaries at regular intervals;

— criteria and methods to be used for evaluating recommendations;

— change-control procedures to enable alterations in the study's scope or content to be made reliably and efficiently.

If consultants are used in the study, they should conform to the same management controls and procedures as in-house personnel.

Many aspects of the study are likely to be investigated in parallel. Full opportunities should be explored in each area, while keeping overall goals within realistic bounds. For example, the organisational, social and personal needs that define desirable applications facilities should not be overly constrained too soon by perceived economic and technical limitations. Similarly, economic costs and benefits should be analysed objectively, without preconceived biases towards favouring particular applications or technical approaches.

In the past, technical aspects have often been allowed to become too dominant in feasibility studies. Many participants in the study have frequently been overawed and/or mystified by IS professionals. Technical specifications have then shaped applications and economic approaches, rather than being shaped by them. The information management approach outlined in this book, with joint project and development teams under business management direction, should avoid this unnecessary bias.

APPLICATIONS REQUIREMENTS

The applications functions that should be performed by an information system are determined by organisational, business and human requirements. Few enterprises are in the position of starting from scratch, so the first task is to examine the existing system. Even if a radical new system is envisaged, information on current practice is necessary to provide a baseline in planning the transition to an innovative future.

If it is a 'green fields' system, building on virgin territory, a distinction must still be made between reasonably predictable immediate circumstances and longer term possibilities.

Examining the Existing System

Four main kinds of functional aspects should be considered: quantifiable, qualitative, formal and informal.

Quantitative parameters include:

— number of each type of document produced, received or transmitted (management reports, performance summaries, memos, letters, work schedules, mail-shots, invoices, bank statements, shelf labels in a shop, photocopies, technical drawings, standard printed forms, etc);

— breakdown of communications costs by medium (telephone, mail, travel, etc), type of communication (voice, data, electronic mail, fax, teleconferencing, car radio, etc) and volumes channelled through each medium (number of telephone calls, mail items, etc);

— volume of words stored and processed (total size of files, numbers and lengths of records and fields within different file types, number of words in various types of document, number and size of drawings produced, etc);

— amounts used of each storage medium (computer disks and tapes, paper, microfiche, video tape, film, etc);

— number of each type of transaction performed (orders taken, queries answered, questions asked, bookings made, customers dealt with at a sales checkout, items processed on a production line, files and records updated, etc);

— sources of information, identifying volumes, types of data and transactions involved with each one;

— number and costs of staff, broken down according to various staff levels and/or work activities.

Qualitative factors are less easy to quantify, although relevant measures are usually possible. They include:

— job satisfaction (staff motivation, problems at the workplace, what increases or reduces morale, etc);

— attitudes to IT (perceptions and understanding of the technology, past experiences, sources of negative attitudes, variations between different groups, etc);

— quality of work (decision-making effectiveness, friendliness and efficiency of customer service, dedication to producing good products, responsiveness to customers' requests, overall management control, etc);

— creative and innovative attitudes (fear of taking a risk, degree of discretion allowed by management, rewards or penalties for going beyond traditional norms, flexibility of organisational structures, etc).

Formal activities are those which conform to official rules and procedures, such as:

— organisational structures (departmental demarcations, management chains of command, reporting lines of communication, job responsibilities, relationships between corporate and local authority, etc);

— management controls (budgeting mechanisms, financial and accounting procedures, performance monitoring requirements, profit and/or service-level targets, extent of consultation expected before decisions taken, quality assurance systems, etc);

— working methods (job descriptions, procedure guidelines, operational task instructions, performance assessment criteria, degree of discretion allowed in performing tasks, etc);

— corporate and external requirements (legal constraints, guidelines for contracts with external suppliers, industrial relations agreements, health and safety legislation, international trading protocols, etc).

Informal features of organisational behaviour were discussed in Chapter 3. They represent the ways in which people work together, perform tasks, exchange information, make decisions and wield power, other than through the formal procedures. Informal aspects are likely to be of significance in areas like:

— inter-personal and inter-group relationships (management/staff, staff/customer, corporate/local, inter-departmental, between management levels, individuals, with external bodies, etc);

— communications (local grapevines, at social meeting places, via informal working contacts, etc);

— decision-making and power politics (cliques, groups loyal to a particular person or tradition, strong personalities, etc).

Predicting the Future

The feasibility study is concerned with more than just investigating the current and traditional situation. It must also determine the best way of proceeding in the future. This involves trying to make realistic predictions about future patterns in many of the areas already discussed, such as:

— changes in the volume of different types of information;

— changes in the number of different types of transaction;

— variations in the location of different activities;

— likely patterns of customer demand for products and services;

— likely patterns of skills requirements and availability of people to satisfy them;

— adaptations and innovations in organisational structure and management style;

— possible mergers, takeovers and coalitions with other organisations.

The success of IS developments frequently depends on making associated changes in organisational structure, management and staff skills and other aspects not directly related to the technology. That is why the need to consider organisation, personal, economic and technical angles in parallel is stressed in this chapter.

COSTS AND BENEFITS

One of the most difficult IS management tasks is to predict the real costs and benefits of a system. There are many 'hidden' costs beyond the basic hardware and software price tags, such as staff training, management time, support, and conversion requirements. If costs are underestimated, disillusionment can set in quickly. On the other hand, a full tabulation of expected costs can cause an unnecessary reluctance to proceed, particularly if the likely benefits are intangible. Attempts to cut costs and go for a cheap solution can lead to severe limitations on the benefits eventually achieved. Significant key benefits often become apparent only after the system has been installed.

It is right for managers and financial controllers to ask what the bottom line *Return On Investment* (*ROI*) is likely to be for an IS development. They should, however, be sensitive to the complexities involved in making calculations and to the inevitable uncertainties in future predictions. The way to minimise these risks is by following the systematic information management approach outlined in the book, rather than by trying to cut costs unjustifiably.

Evaluating IS Investments

There are two main focal points for analysing costs and benefits: *cost substitution* or *value-added*. Cost substitution is concerned primarily with seeking to replace one set of resources, such as people, with a cheaper resource, typically a computer system. The value-added perspective looks for broader and more imaginative benefits that can accrue from an IS investment, such as new products and services or radically different ways of running a business.

It is easier to quantify cost substitution than value-added approaches. They should, however, be regarded as complementary techniques that coexist on all developments. If either one is allowed to dominate unnecessarily, mistakes will be made. An obsession with cost substitution can restrict management vision and the eventual range of benefits obtained. An excessive concentration on value-added gains could lead to ambitious projects being launched on brittle financial foundations.

Traditional DP investments were predominantly based on cost substitution analyses. One of the most commonly used means of computer justifications has been the *Discounted Cash Flow* (*DCF*) technique. This relies on a quantification of likely costs and benefits over a number of years to work out how long an investment will take to pay for itself. It is biased towards investments that bring short-term benefits with clear-cut outcomes.

DCF works reasonably well with the kinds of routine administrative applications that formed the core of traditional mainframe DP activities. Word processing, order entry and other secretarial and clerical systems come out even more favourably from DCF analyses. The system's costs for these applications are relatively low — and falling; people costs are high in comparison — and getting higher.

The limitations of the cost substitution view have been highlighted by the growing IT convergence of the 1980s. Integrated information systems pervade many areas of an organisation's operations. As Michael Porter's value-chain framework has shown (see Chapter 3), an IS innovation in one activity can have widespread impacts elsewhere.

This raises important issues about the organisational structures used in evaluating IS investment decisions. For management control purposes, it is usually preferable to have a sponsoring department which controls the budget for a project. There is a natural tendency for that department to give priority to benefits within its organisational boundary. Impacts in other parts of the value-chain may then receive insufficient attention. Organisational guidelines should, therefore, insist that a corporate perspective is taken when assessing IS developments. Where necessary, costs should be shared equitably, even though the bulk of an investment may come from the sponsoring department's budget. The cost of building the IS infrastructure should be viewed as a corporate asset with long-term potential, so should be funded accordingly.

Many key IS applications would never get off the ground without a corporate perspective. For example, substantial benefits from an EPOS system accrue in warehousing distribution, purchasing, marketing, accounting and other activities, in addition to the retail operations for which electronic point-of-sale terminals are most directly needed. Taking into account these non-retail advantages will justify much greater expenditure on the network, including the IS infrastructure to support it, than if retail requirements alone are the main criteria.

Economic Assessment Techniques

The following are some of the approaches and concepts that should be considered in deciding how to assess IS costs and benefits:

> *Quantified Cost-Benefit Analysis* (*CBA*). This focuses primarily on cost substitution and cost avoidance issues, using approaches like DCF. Analyses should be sensitive to the many factors, and their interactions, which influence outcomes, including relevant measures of qualitative aspects. For example, an *improved customer service* can be judged in terms of the time taken to fulfil a product order or to answer customer queries; *improved job satisfaction* can be related to staff turnover, absenteeism and error rates. Weightings should be assigned to each factor to distinguish between different user and business priorities.

> *Long-term payoffs*. Many investments, such as in IS infrastructure and training programmes, are not suited to CBA techniques which expect paybacks to be delivered in a few years, rather than over a five-ten year period, or longer.

Value-chain analysis. An investigation must be made of the ripple effect of an investment or project throughout the organisation, including the distribution of costs and benefits between different activities and functional units.

Restructuring and innovation impacts. Many important business benefits arise when the introduction of a new system is associated with organisational restructuring or other significant innovations. However, the results of major restructuring and innovation initiatives are the most difficult to predict; they are often high-risk, high-payoff ventures. A systematic attempt must be made, nevertheless, to try to estimate their effects, such as the changing value of particular job functions and departments after restructuring, or the risks and costs involved in trying to gain competitive advantage by being first with a new IT facility.

Timing and phasing of investments. The time when an investment starts, and the level of funding provided in different phases, can have important effects on the pattern of benefits achieved. A delay in making a decision to go ahead with a project, or the provision of too little funding in the early phases, can waste benefits by failing to deliver them quickly enough. An analysis should be made of how to accelerate the achievement of benefits, without rushing too quickly and massively into poorly prepared projects.

The balance between these aspects will vary according to the nature of an application or development. They should all be borne in mind to help develop a complete picture of likely future results.

Important Cost Considerations

In assessing IS investments, the following are some key costs to be taken into account:

— direct prices of hardware and software;

— telecommunications costs;

— maintenance and support (by outside vendors and/or in-house specialists) necessary to provide an effective, continuing service;

— accessories, consumables, and ancillary equipment (floppy disks, printer ribbons, magnetic tape racks, new furniture suited to ergonomic operation of computer workstations, special paper and stationery, cabling, acoustic hoods for printers, uninterruptable power supplies, etc);

— using a *bureau*, which charges for access to its hardware and software, if necessary;

— IS project management and development costs (design, analysis, programming, etc);

— recruitment, training and salaries of IS specialists;

— use of outside consultants and contractors;

— training of non-IS staff in understanding and using the new system;

— time spent by non-IS management and staff evaluating, developing, introducing and sorting out operational problems;

— site preparation and changes to the built environment;

— transition and conversion costs (rewriting software for new hardware, establishing computer files or databases for the first time, converting existing data formats to those needed by the new system, parallel operation of the existing system until the new one is fully operational, the employment of temporary staff to cope with any extra work during the transition, etc);

— installation and delivery charges required by some suppliers;

— ongoing operational costs;

— one-off payments to encourage staff to move to a new system, or redundancy payments, if applicable;

— insurance of equipment and of the 'consequential loss' if the service is interrupted for a significant period;

— backup equipment and services in the case of system failure or damage to an installation, which may include the availability of off-site disk and tape stores and standby systems with capabilities for running key workloads;

— the cost of documentation, including regular updating;

— the cost of software and hardware upgrades;

— the cost of having a system with limited growth opportunity, or which fails to adhere to widely used standards;

— the cost of *in*efficiency (excessive inventory, poor cash flow, lack of timely and accurate information for management decision-making, etc);

— the cost of delaying the introduction of a system, thereby losing a period in which benefits would have accrued;

— the cost of failure if the system works inefficiently or breaks down frequently;

— the cost, in monetary and human terms, of failing to take adequate account of the quality of the working environment during the transition and after the new system is operational.

Potential Benefits

The following are some of the benefits that should be looked for from a new information system:

— added value for existing products and customer/client services;

— new products and services;

— savings on staff, equipment and services employed in existing systems;

— improved productivity;

— reduced stock levels;

— less office space needed to store paper-based information;

— more responsive production techniques, such as flexible manufacturing methods;

— faster, more efficient and varied telecommunications options (computer networking, electronic mail, fax, advanced telephony, etc);

— quicker access to more accurate and timely management information about the performance of particular business units, groups and individuals, such as cash flows, sales trends, customer problems, work productivity, progress on production lines, etc;

— better information on competitive market positions and other external developments;

— better management planning and forecasting;

— more flexibility in the location of offices, facilities and people;

— enhanced quality of the working environment;

— automation of routine tasks, leaving more time for management and staff to spend on creative, caring and other more valuable activities;

— improved ability to organise and control international and global operations;

— gaining of competitive advantages;

— increased profits in the private sector, more cost-effective services in the public sector.

TECHNICAL REQUIREMENTS

Assessing technical aspects of an information system is the most daunting prospect facing business managers. Non-IS specialists cannot be expected to be fully conversant with every nuance of such a rapidly changing technology. Yet the choice of technological system has a fundamental effect on the benefits gained or lost. Information management methods must ensure, therefore, that IS specialists apply their expertise to meet corporate goals.

The technical feasibility study has been left until last in this discussion not because it is unimportant, but because it must be subservient to organisational, economic, social and personal user requirements. This is the most effective way of ensuring technologists do not drive applications towards inappropriate directions.

Avoiding Unnecessary Jargon

Business managers must insist that IS specialists explain in plain language the reasons for any major technical innovation or departure from corporate IS standards. One of the IS manager's key duties is to ensure technical IS investments are justified in terms that make sense to management colleagues and users.

As in most scientific and technical activities, IS professionals have developed many specialist terms to describe the theory and practice of their discipline. Although this may appear to be confusing jargon to outsiders, it is a useful and necessary part of communications between experts. The dividing line between what is regarded as jargon and what are 'everyday' words is also constantly shifting. For example, at one time *hardware, software, word processors* and *personal computers* were regarded as jargon; now the terms are widely understood.

The main problem arises when IS professionals communicate with non-specialists. In some cases, inherent technical complexities and subtleties make it genuinely very difficult to explain IT concepts and facilities in plain language. Frequently, however, IS experts find it difficult to avoid unnecessary jargon or to explain key terms simply. Like many other technical specialists, they may often be poor communicators who cannot break from the jargon habit that has become ingrained in their daily working lives.

A concerted effort is therefore needed to overcome these problems. Understandable explanations of technical matters must be explicitly requested where relevant. Training in communication with the 'outside world' should be given to IS professionals who need to be able to do so. If necessary, communication experts should be employed to write documents and generally interface between IS specialists and the rest of the organisation. The feasibility study is a crucial area where technical requirements need to be translated into objectives, facilities, and plans that can be understood by general management.

Defining Technical Facilities

Many technical requirements flow from the applications and economic analyses already discussed. For example, applications requirements define the technical systems performance that must be provided and indicate the kinds of systems and architectures that will be appropriate.

The following are some of the main technical aspects that must be considered, in the context of business, user and economic objectives:

— performance targets, such as the speed with which tasks must be carried out and the level of reliability expected;

— the overall configuration and architecture, including the numbers and locations of users and workstations, data centres, data-bases/data files, printers, etc;

— telecommunications routes and volumes between various locations and users, which will be needed to help specify the optimum communications architecture;

— *transaction analyses* to determine the numbers and types of transactions to be carried out (file updates, file enquiries, the volume of information associated with each transaction, etc);

— amount and type of data storage needed to take account of information volumes, file sizes, etc;

— *data modelling* to analyse the types of data used, relationships between data items, access paths through a database for different transactions, relative amounts of activity that can be expected for different data items and other factors which are needed to decide on the most appropriate database or file management method to use;

— *process modelling* to analyse the routines used for processing information, their frequency of performance, interactions between them, etc;

— inputs to the system, including the numbers and categories of inputs and their sources (customers making an order, point-of-sale transactions, signals from sensors, etc), types of information involved (printed text and diagrams, telephone calls, handwriting, standard forms, etc), media used (direct input from terminals, external mail, telecommunications links, etc), locations of input sources, frequencies and volumes associated with each type of input;

— outputs from the systems, including the numbers and categories of outputs (reports, documents, messages, signals, etc), types of information involved (text, graphics, combined graphics and text, computer data, voice, etc), media to be used (paper, screen displays, etc), locations where output is needed, frequencies and volumes associated with each type of output, etc;

— user/system interactions which determine the hardware and software interfaces that enable systems to be used with optimum ease, comfort and efficiency;

— security and audit control covering access to information in databases, recording transactions to guard against fraud, attention to legislation (including data protection laws), standby and backup facilities, and other safeguards against theft, spying, sabotage, accidents, etc;

— priorities to weight the relative importance of different activities, types of report, classes of data, etc.

In each of these categories, estimates are needed of requirements immediately after the new system becomes operational and long-term usage predictions. Even though future demand is always difficult to predict precisely, realistic projections are essential in order to carry out two key activities effectively:

— *sizing* a system to ensure sufficient facilities are available to handle operational workloads (number of terminals, processing power, data storage capacity, etc);

— *capacity planning* to cater for workload evolution and growth (see Chapter 12 for more about capacity management).

PRESENTING FEASIBILITY STUDY RESULTS

Progress reports on all phases and aspects of feasibility studies should be an integral part of the IS plan. These reports must be presented in a form that can be readily evaluated by all the people affected, including non-IS specialists. The final report must relate back to the objectives set in the original terms of reference, as amended through appropriate change-control procedures.

A typical final report should include:

— *a management summary* in plain language, to highlight overall conclusions and recommendations;

— *the scope of the study*, specifying applications and activities investigated;

— *terms of reference analysis*, showing which aspects of the original terms have been fulfilled and the reasons why some objectives were changed or not fulfilled;

— *the nature of existing information systems*: work procedures, equipment, staff, inefficiencies, etc;

— *the advantages/disadvantages of existing system*, explaining which aspects are to be retained, if any;

— *an outline proposal for the new information system*, explaining how it: overcomes inadequacies in the existing system, maintains or improves on the existing system's advantages, introduces new benefits, etc;

— *the applications priorities* to distinguish key business systems from secondary ones;

— *the costs, procedures and schedules* for changing to the new information system;

— *the impact of the new system on organisational, social and personal factors*, summarising the main benefits and disadvantages, opportunities and problems;

— *economic assessments*, summarising key CBA, value-chain analysis and other evaluations;

— *the alternatives considered* and reasons for their rejection;

— *overall technical recommendations;*

— *personnel and training recommendations;*

— *summary resource estimates* phased over defined periods: costs, people, capital investments, space, etc;

— *external factors* that might affect outcomes and how they can be dealt with, for example: technological innovations, new services from a telecommunications supplier, standardisation agreements or government legislation.

The size and nature of the report will depend upon the scope of the project and the target audiences. It is generally a good practice to produce a succinct and readable main report, with extra detail provided in separate reports or appendices.

SUMMARY: LAYING THE FOUNDATIONS

This chapter has described the purposes of feasibility studies, how they should be managed and the key factors that they should investigate. Emphasis has been placed on giving precedence to business and user applications needs. This involves:

— setting terms of reference that make explicit the need to cover a full range of organisational, social, personal, economic and technical factors;

— managing the study by a balanced team of corporate, user and IS representatives;

— insisting that IS experts explain key technological factors in plain language;

— objectively exploring the existing systems, highlighting advantages as well as constraints;

— giving as much weight to qualitative, informal and often intangible factors, as well as more formal and easily quantifiable ingredients;

— planning for change and evolution in the long term;

— providing a clear business focus to all developments;

— bearing in mind at all stages that objectives set in feasibility studies become criteria against which success or failure is judged throughout the life cycle of the resultant system.

Once a decision has been taken to go ahead, the feasibility study provides the basis for specifying the operational requirements, which will be used in looking for suitable systems and designing an appropriate solution.

9 Finding Appropriate Solutions

OPERATIONAL REQUIREMENTS

The system requirements that result from a feasibility study could be met by:

— enhancing existing hardware and software;

— obtaining new hardware and/or software from existing suppliers;

— going to new suppliers or, at least, to ask new suppliers to tender for the work;

— significant software and systems development by in-house IS professionals;

— employment of consultants and other specialists to develop tailor-made systems;

— a combination of these solutions.

The development of an operational requirement specification is a precursor to any of these steps. If new suppliers are to be sought, tenders need to be drawn up and responses evaluated. Practical issues like financing new systems also need to be considered. These aspects are examined in this chapter. Managing in-house developments is discussed in Chapter 10.

Defining System Capabilities

The operational requirement follows from the context set by the workload and technical performance criteria discussed in Chapter 8 (frequency and sources of different transactions, types and volumes of telecommunications traffic and the routes they go along, numbers and locations of users, etc). The operational criteria that can be extrapolated from these characteristics include:

125

— numbers, locations and capabilities of computers (mainframes, minis, PCs, etc), workstations, terminals, data centres, printers and other major system resources;

— storage and memory requirements (main memory, hard disk, floppy disk, tape, etc);

— minimum response time (speed of responding to an enquiry or other input at a workstation) when the maximum number of workstations is in operation;

— minimum number of workstations and terminals to be supported by a multi-user system, while still giving acceptable performance;

— communications and network architecture(s);

— the 'core' tasks at the heart of the application which must be dealt with most efficiently, which help to decide whether certain specialised capabilities are needed, such as a dedicated word processor rather than a general-purpose PC in an office application;

— any special applications that may need a different solution to the rest of the system, say using a stand-alone PC package rather than a multi-user system for certain tasks;

— *availability* of overall system (percentage of time available for useful work);

— *reliability* of discrete parts of the system, such as networks, mainframes, workstations, PCs, printers, etc, measured usually in terms of *Mean Time Between Failures* (*MTBFs*);

— *resilience* (speed and efficiency of recovery from failures) of the overall system;

— types and numbers of specialist input and output devices needed (EPOS terminals, handwriting or voice recognition units, laser printers, etc);

— service-call response times and regularity of routine maintenance.

Other general IS policy guidelines that may have to be taken into account include:

— compatibility with technical standards specified in the IS strategy, unless there is a convincing reason for a waiver, say because a particular specialised system is best met by a non-standard system or because there is an overriding need to remain compatible with an existing non-standard system;

— compatibility with existing hardware, operating systems or other key prior investments;

— flexibility to ensure the system can be enhanced and adapted over a long period to meet evolving applications needs;

— effective and efficient support (maintenance, training, document-ation, etc);

— availability of alternative suppliers (of software, hardware, maint-enance, etc).

Making Requirements Realistic

One of the important causes of IS headaches has been that systems which meet theoretical operational requirements fail to deliver the goods in practice. This danger can be minimised by following the approach to supplier and system selection discussed later in the chapter. In addition, the operational requirements specification must be designed to emphasise realistic performance criteria. For example, suppliers of multi-user systems often quote the theoretical maximum number of users that can be attached to a system, in terms like "Up to x workstations can be attached". At the same time, they tend to quote 'starting' prices based on the minimum amount of memory and processing power provided. In practice, it is usually found that much more than the minimum capability and price is needed for a working system, while performance deteriorates unacceptably as the maximum number of attached users is reached.

The operational requirements should, therefore, be careful in defining the numbers of users and expected performance that will be the norm in live usage. The fear of poor performance should not, however, lead to *over-specification*, for example, by taking the maximum number of online users (which may be a rare occurrence) as the norm. This can lead to obtaining a much too powerful and expensive system.

A particularly tricky aspect of defining operational requirements is predicting future demand. If a system is extremely successful, it may quickly hit the upper performance targets. The best way of protecting against this possibility is through giving priority to standardisation policies and to investigating the smooth growth potential of a system.

Adherence to standards opens possibilities for having a wider range of alternative suppliers for different parts of the system, which can facilitate the enhancement of a system when performance limits are reached. The growth path of a particular system indicates how easy and efficient it will be to extend capabilities over a long period.

HUMAN FACTORS REQUIREMENTS

A crucial ingredient in the operational requirement should be human factors specifications, identifying the characteristics that will make the system easy to understand and simple, efficient and comfortable to operate. However, despite their importance, human factors are often treated partially, or virtually ignored, in operational specifications.

Human factors should be treated as systematically and comprehensively as any other aspect of operational requirements. Many human factors needs will arise from the applications feasibility study, which investigates how the system should perform and what users should do with it. Others will be included in general policy guidelines and standards, such as those relating to physical ergonomic design and work practices. The two main human factors aspects that should be covered in operational requirements are user/system interactions and the ergonomic design of physical equipment. Key general human factors aspects that should be used in assessing user interfaces include:

— *Comprehensibility*: the ease with which relevant users can understand what the system is doing and how it functions;

— *Convenience*: the simplicity, efficiency and reliability with which the system is operated;

— *Adaptability*: the extent, efficiency and ease with which the system can be adjusted to meet the changing needs of particular users or the different needs of various types of user;

— *Consistency*: the maintenance of compatible interface concepts and techniques across different tasks, and when the system is enhanced to meet new applications requirements;

— *Precision*: avoidance of ambiguity in information content and necessary user actions;

— *Tolerance*: the degree to which the system is tolerant of users making slight variations and errors in interactions;

— *Aptness*: how well system interactions fit users' natural perceptions of how tasks should be carried out and the comfort with which they can do it;

— *Helpfulness*: the amount of support given to assist users in performing required tasks;

— *Friendliness*: the politeness of messages and dialogues.

Some suppliers have latched onto the phrase 'user friendliness' to imply a system has good human factors standards. 'Friendliness', however, is just one desirable characteristic. It is possible to have a superficially friendly interface that is also inflexible, ambiguous, inconsistent, intolerant and unhelpful. Basic systems design criteria, like adaptability, smooth evolutionary growth, fast response times and high availability, contribute to maintaining appropriate user interfaces.

There are two main constituents of user/system interaction: the *task interface*, which is how hardware and software combine to help carry out particular tasks, and the *ergonomic hardware design* of workstations and terminals.

The Task Interface

Many innovations in workstation designs have been motivated by the desire to make the task interface as natural as possible. For example, the window, icon, menu, pointer (WIMP) approach discussed in Chapter 1 aims to make a workstation screen act like an office desk top, on which many documents can be displayed and multiple tasks carried out. Other new forms of input and output also make systems more natural to use, say through handwriting or voice recognition systems and *touch-sensitive screens* that users touch at the relevant place to indicate their response or the action to be initiated.

The following task-interface features implement the general human factors requirements summarised above:

— *user profiling*, which enables the system to be tailored to particular users' needs and to be adapted over time as users' needs evolve;

— *easily memorised task initiation and operation*, so that the user does not have to refer to other documents frequently to find out what to do next;

— *avoidance of error-prone functions*, for example, where damaging consequences can result from a simple mistyping or pressing the 'erase' key mistakenly because it has been positioned close to other frequently-used keys;

— *ensuring the user always knows what to do next*;

— *clear, easily understandable information presentation* on screens, in printouts, etc;

— *messages that are polite and informative, not rude and curt;*

— *keeping the user informed of what is happening at all times*: for example, if there is likely to be a significant delay in response times or the system is unavailable for a particular reason;

— *efficient and helpful trapping and reporting of errors*, indicating, wherever possible, what has gone wrong and what, if anything, the user can do to correct it;

— *help facilities that are meaningful* in the context of the task being performed;

— *clean interrupts*, so that if the user wants to stop work for a time or there is a breakdown in the system, a restart can be made easily from the point at which work was interrupted, without any information having been lost in the interim;

— *different facilities for novices and experienced users;*

— *WYSIWYG* — *what you see is what you get*, pronounced 'whizzywig', to ensure that the way information is shown on a screen is similar to how it will be presented in printed output;

— *unobtrusiveness of the operating system*, allowing the user to focus completely on the application task in hand.

Hardware Ergonomics

The operation and handling of physical devices is an intrinsic part of user/system interaction. Hardware ergonomic design follows the same principles of comprehensibility, convenience, adaptability, aptness, etc, as for other human factors aspects.

The operation of all equipment should be easy to understand and manipulate, whether it is putting paper in a printer, fitting a floppy disk into a drive or working a powerful graphics workstation. Particular attention has been given to screen-based workstations because they are so essential to most activities. Flexibility is a high priority in screen and keyboard designs. That is why it is recommended that the screen and keyboard are separate, so that each can be positioned in the most convenient place for a particular working situation.

Important ergonomic screen characteristics include the stability, brightness and legibility of characters. Images on the screen are formed by electronic beams from a *Cathode Ray Tube* (*CRT*) hitting an inner coating of phosphor on the screen. The image fades as soon as it is formed, so has to be refreshed quickly. The *refresh rate* affects the stability of the characters on the screen; rates of about 60 Hertz (Hz) for light characters on a dark background and 80 Hz for black-on-white are regarded as optimum for avoiding character flicker.

It is important that easily accessible brightness controls are available because ambient lighting varies so much. Screens should also have an anti-reflection coating or filter to avoid glare. The siting of screens in relation to natural and artificial lighting can exacerbate these screen problems. Images on the screen should be easy to read and unambiguous; for example, there should be clear distinctions between items that could be confused, like 2 and Z.

The keyboard should be designed to aid operator comfort and efficiency. For example, labels on keys should be easily legible and clearly indicate the function performed. Numeric keypads and other special function keys may need to be highlighted by being in a different colour or special position.

Consideration should also be given to the desks and chairs used with workstations. Chairs should have adjustable height and back-support controls, and good stability. Desks should be a comfortable height with sufficient space for the workstation and related equipment, like document holders. The viewing distance from the screen when the operator is seated should minimise eye strain (about 35 to 70 cm is acceptable).

TYPES OF SUPPLIER

In some cases, operational requirements can be met purely by existing suppliers and systems and/or in-house IS developments. If there is a need to look for new suppliers and systems, considerable care and attention must be given to the selection process. A new supplier may be required for the complete system or only parts of it. Existing hardware may be retained, but new software sought for it. The expansion of an existing network could mean that an independent maintenance company is needed because the hardware supplier(s) and in-house IS specialists can no longer service it satisfactorily. A number of types of supplier could be considered:

— *hardware manufacturers* who supply equipment directly to users;

— *plug-compatible and lookalike manufacturers* who supply hardware that meets the same external interfaces as systems from major manufacturers, such as the wide variety of PCs compatible with IBM personal computers;

— *Other Equipment Manufacturers (OEMs) and 'badge-engineered' suppliers* who offer systems under their own names of which part, or all, of the major components or computers come from other manufacturers;

— *software product companies and software houses* who market the products they have developed, directly to users;

— *dealers and agents* who sell, on commission, hardware and software from other suppliers, without doing much development of their own;

— *Value-Added Resellers (VARs)*, who are similar to dealers, but who provide additional products and services to enhance the capabilities of the original system;

— *second-hand* suppliers of used hardware;

— *systems houses* who develop complete systems tailored to individual user needs and who may also offer a variety of other products and services;

— *consultancies* who primarily advise users on how to manage, select and implement information systems, which may include the provision of specific management and development methodologies, techniques and tools;

— *bureaux* who offer access to their own computer facilities, which means that a user could get the benefits of IT for particular applications without installing an in-house system to process the workload;

— *facilities management* companies who take over the control of all, or part, of an organisation's computing capabilities or IS function;

— *systems integration* companies who take prime contractual responsibility for supplying a totally integrated system, made up from products and services from a number of vendors;

— *contract staff agencies* who provide IS specialists for a defined period;

— *education and training* companies who offer skills training at their own centres or on the customer's premises;

— *technical writing agencies* who supply technical writers for specific contracts;

— *recruitment agencies* who assist in obtaining IS specialists with required skills;

— *independent third-party maintenance companies* who provide an alternative source of support to product suppliers.

External Management and Service Options

Most of this book is oriented towards advising managers how to define, choose, develop and run information systems of their own. There are, however, many circumstances in which all or part of the responsibility for this process could best be taken over by an external IT services company (such as a bureau, facilities management company or systems integration specialist).

Bureaux

Bureaux were more popular when the only computers on the market were large and expensive. They enabled organisations to access costly computer power at an economical rate. Some bureaux pioneered online services, originally known as time sharing. However, with the growing availability of lower-cost computing, bureaux have concentrated more on providing specialised services and expertise in particular applications, as well as access to large-scale computing capabilities.

A bureau could be a desirable option where such skills and resources cannot be provided in-house in a more cost-effective way. Bureaux can also be useful in handling peak workloads, say during conversion to a new system, or for smaller companies that do not have sufficient money or the skilled resources to warrant systems of their own. Using a bureau also relieves an organisation of the responsibility for supporting and maintaining systems.

Bureaux charge primarily for the computer processing time and storage space allocated to a user. One of the difficulties in evaluating bureaux cost/benefits is predicting the size of workloads. Other costs may involve input/output transfers to the bureau (manually or by telecommunications), consultancy advice and the use of certain software packages.

Facilities Management and Systems Integration

Facilities management and systems integration services range from providing project management assistance, to taking complete control of a system's development or the operation of a data centre. These services are of particular value to organisations who lack the necessary skills, and can provide effective cost controls. On the other hand, they give an outside organisation a key role in important internal activities and removes important opportunities for in-house staff to gain more IS managerial experience.

Independent Maintenance Companies

For networks covering many locations, independent maintenance companies can often offer a more effective support service than could be provided by the in-house IS department or product suppliers. For example, larger maintenance companies can afford the investments needed to build up the service centres, multi-product expertise, spares supplies and skilled engineering resources necessary to service a nationwide network.

SELECTING SUPPLIERS AND SYSTEMS

Each type of supplier will have its own selection criteria that have to be investigated. There are, however, important general principles that apply to the process of inviting tenders and evaluating responses from any IS suppliers.

The Invitation to Tender

The search for a suitable supplier is unlikely to begin only when the feasibility study has been completed. During the study, there will probably be a continuous scanning of the market to find relevant systems. There should also be discussions with some suppliers, which may help to keep the study within realistic bounds. The aim in drawing up a list of the suppliers who will be sent tenders is to include a good mix of potential candidates, without having so many that evaluating responses becomes an onerous and tedious task.

If there is a preferred supplier policy (see Chapter 6), the choice will be limited for certain systems and services, unless there is a strong case for looking wider. Even with a preferred supplier policy which covers the main hardware systems, there can be a considerable degree of freedom in looking for suppliers of compatible software and hardware.

Much useful information can be gleaned from suppliers' brochures and other literature. Although some of this must be treated with caution because it is primarily designed as sales promotional material, a good idea can be obtained of whether or not it is worth considering the supplier or system further. Reports in the IT press and specialist IT sections of the general media, together with visits to relevant conferences and exhibitions, can also be of value in deciding who should be invited to tender.

The tender document itself should include all key performance measures that will have to be met. The focus must be on the main 'core' needs, although any other important, but subsidiary, issues also have to be mentioned. It should specify basic facts, such as:

— brief background on the user's organisation, showing where the particular system being tendered for fits into the overall corporate structure;

— a short summary of objectives and scope of the tender;

— a summary of prime operational requirements that should be met, including support services needed (a detailed specification could be added as an appendix);

— guidelines on acceptable cost parameters, including an indication of how the system is likely to be financed (purchase, lease, rent, etc);

— the procedures and schedules involved in selecting a supplier;

— the implementation schedules expected;

— an outline of the contents the user wants to be covered in the final contract.

In addition, the tender should request information about the supplier's commercial and business viability, like:

— the latest company financial report;

— any other supporting information to indicate its general financial stability (special evidence may be needed for new companies);

— basic company details, such as length of time in business, size, main areas of expertise, special qualities of principals and other professionals (of particular relevance to consultancies and to new companies);

— any link with another company that may bias the proposal (such as a tie-up between a consultant and a hardware or software supplier);

— the percentage of a supplier's business devoted to the type of system or service proposed;

— the number of users/installed versions of the system or service proposed, broken down by geographic region and/or industry sectors;

— the total number of users of the suppliers' systems and services;

— the number of professional staff employed in the relevant application area or system/service;

— the number and location of support staff and service centres;

— details of any relevant user group(s);

— the name of some users who can be contacted;

— information on any special price or support arrangements being offered, say for a new product.

Evaluating Suppliers' Proposals

Assessing technical proposals is the most difficult aspect of choosing between responses to the tender. Paper specifications of a system's performance can be relied on only as a very general guideline as to how the system will perform in practice.

Significant indicators of the 'power' of a system could include the speed of its processor(s), the data transfer rates it can handle internally and the number and throughput rates of its communication channels with external systems. However, simple comparisons between these kinds of measurements can be misleading. For example, the speed of a processor, usually measured in millions of instructions per second (*mips*), may have been relevant for applications on older mainframes with a single Central Processing Unit (CPU) through which all work was routed. Many systems, including mainframes, now have processing power spread through many parts of its architecture: one or more CPUs, disk controllers, communications processors, input/output controllers, database processors, etc. Simply adding up all the 'mips power' in a system does not indicate whether the spread of processing power is ideally balanced for particular kinds of workload. A scientific application, say, may demand high CPU rates because it consists mainly of complex calculations. An online transaction processing system, with many terminals and a large database, depends more on the speed of handling lots of users, transactions, disk accesses, etc. The deployment of processing capabilities to cope with high-speed inputs and outputs will be different for some real-time applications, like telemetry control systems.

A practical demonstration of how the system will deal with a live workload is, therefore, important. Except for small systems, this is usually difficult to do precisely because each workload is likely to be unique and it may be complex and costly, if not impossible, to set up a realistic 'dummy' live workload.

Benchmark tests are a popular way of checking how a system will cope with a representative sample of typical workload mix. There are some industry-standard benchmarks for certain kinds of workload, but users can also specify benchmarks tailored to their own circumstances. One problem with benchmarks is that suppliers can tune their system to the benchmark parameters, so better performance is obtained than would be the case in live operations. If the organisation has its own IS professionals with appropriate expertise, in-house trials can be conducted, rather than relying on the supplier to produce the system which carries out the benchmark test.

A valuable way of assessing how systems perform is to talk to existing users, if possible, ones having similar workload characteristics to the application being assessed. Suppliers should be willing to provide lists of users who can be contacted. There are also often user groups for the supplier of a particular system. Some suppliers, however, may put forward 'tame' users for such contacts. They may select users who have had unusually favourable experiences. The user may even have a vested interest in promoting a particular system because it could have been jointly developed, with the user receiving a royalty for sales. When visiting existing users, these possibilities should be borne in mind.

Practical advice on how a system performs could also be found from user groups associated with an application, industry or profession, instead of supplier-based ones. Meetings of independent user groups and professional bodies can also provide a useful point of contact for informal discussions of actual experiences with a system.

Making a Decision

Arriving at a final decision about a supplier or system involves drawing together a variety of relevant factors. The aim of preparing, issuing and evaluating tenders is to try to give a sound factual basis on which choices can be successfully made.

Tables can be drawn up of key operational requirements and supplier selection criteria, in which each factor is given a 'score'. This could, say, allocate marks on a particular scale (say 0 to 10) or simpler 'High/Medium/Low' assessments. Weightings can be given to factors according to their importance and priority, which ensures final 'totals' take account of the most significant needs.

In the end, however, all relevant selection aspects cannot be reduced to a convenient set of numbers. Qualitative management judgements also have to be made. Advice from IS professionals with practical experience of the pitfalls that often dog systems development and operation is essential; informal discussions with other users can also be helpful in unearthing the reality behind formal proposals. In some cases, it may be necessary to take a risk. The 'safest' decision is usually to choose a well-established supplier and a well-established system or service. This is also frequently the most successful course to follow.

However if this approach was universally adhered to, there would be no opportunity for innovative applications, suppliers, products and services to make their mark. Provided the implications have been thoroughly understood, a decision to 'take a chance' could produce enormous business payoffs. Many of the companies who have gained the most significant advantages from information systems have been adventurous enough to be first with a new application or technological innovation. New suppliers have also often provided the ideas and agility that have given IS users a vital edge over rivals.

Considerable extra effort from managers and IS professionals may be needed for innovatory ventures. The technical aspects have to be learnt; new suppliers must be fully evaluated; the commitment of established suppliers to new approaches must be carefully examined; and mistakes are more probable. Substantial, tangible benefits must, therefore, be clearly identified before taking any risk.

Contingency plans must also be considered in the event of something going wrong. For a large organisation, this could mean being prepared to provide financial support directly to a supplier at some stage. For smaller companies, an alliance with other users could be sought to help share costs and risks.

Development and implementation plans for riskier projects should avoid trying to do too much at the same time, particularly in the early phases. Systematic controls should seek to minimise risks and consequences of failure, without stifling the imaginative impulse that is the *raison d'être* for taking a risk in the first place.

NEGOTIATING THE CONTRACT

The contract between a customer and IS supplier is more than just a legal necessity. It can be an important management tool for imposing a disciplined approach to the introduction of a new system or service and the resolution of disputes. Therefore, senior management should be involved in the process of negotiating a contract and not leave it to legal and technical experts.

Many suppliers have their own standard contracts which they seek to impose on all users. These are often biased towards the suppliers' rights. Even if a supplier's standard contract is used as the basis for negotiations, users must ensure their rights are also protected.

Many systems have more than one key supplier. The main computer hardware, operating system, applications software, disk drives, printers and other key elements of the system could each come from a different company. Yet the effectiveness of the overall system depends on all elements working together. This can add an important extra dimension to contract negotiations.

What A Contract Should Contain

The essence of a contract is to make explicit, in unambiguous terms, the responsibilities, expectations and liabilities for all parties concerned. Nothing should be left to chance and the small print must be read carefully. It is dangerous to assume that there may be implicit safeguards that need not be referred to directly.

Many information systems are complex technical entities that are subject to frequent changes. There can be many intricate arguments about the cause of faults, particularly if many suppliers are involved. If necessary, specialist advice on contracts should be obtained from consultants and relevant professional bodies. The following are important issues that could be part of contract negotiations:

— all key performance and specification criteria;

— definitions of who is responsible for each activity at various times (during development, pre- and post-installation, pre- and post-acceptance testing, when enhancements are made and new versions or models introduced, etc);

— definition of responsibilities relating to the provision of correct information by each party;

— the precise obligations on each party if they fail to meet their responsibilities, such as the supplier overcoming performance shortfalls by offering extra hardware or software, either free or at reduced cost, or the customer agreeing to pay costs incurred by the provision of incorrect information;

— full details of any warranties covering complete systems and services, or discrete elements within them;

— complete listing of subsidiary as well as main costs, for example charges made by the supplier for in-situ installation, rather than simply delivering a system 'to the door';

— acceptance by the supplier that systems will be delivered only after the customer has given permission, to avoid the kind of situations which have occurred when goods have been delivered without customers being ready for them;

— the form of protection given if the supplier goes out of business or is taken over, such as access to relevant software codes, documentation and other information needed to keep the system operational;

— circumstances in which the contract can be cancelled by either party;

— clarification of responsibilities, obligations, rights of access, etc, when a number of suppliers are involved, including details of any extra charges made by a supplier to support systems in a mixed vendor environment and any restrictions a supplier wants to impose on mixing systems (or an agreement to have no restrictions);

— requirements for the provision of appropriate documentation;

— details of all support and maintenance capabilities expected, including regular updates and continuing supplies of hardware, software and documentation;

— clarification of the ownership of software, particularly where it has been jointly developed with a supplier;

— explanation of how software copyright is to be protected, for example if a software licence relates to one machine or a large number in a network, and what the customer must do if software is to be moved to a machine for which the licence does not apply;

— procedures to govern variations in the contract, with guidelines for the allocation of costs and liabilities if changes are deemed to be unreasonable by either side.

Keeping the Contract Realistic

No contract can guarantee against problems arising between customers and suppliers. However, the number of disputes, and the ease of resolving them, can be greatly reduced by using the contract to deal with areas of possible contention at an early stage, taking into account the actual nature of information systems. For example, it is probably unrealistic to expect most new software to be completely bug-free. It may, therefore, be sensible to have a clause in the contract which allows the customer to accept a system subject to the correction of faults at a later date, provided the system delivers a service that is of an acceptable standard in the interim and a timetable is set for providing a full service.

The genuine difficulties of assigning 'blame' between users and suppliers for faults should be acknowledged, without preventing stipulations that the supplier should maintain required performance levels. In many cases, problems do arise because users have provided inadequate requirement specifications or operate the system incorrectly. There are, however, circumstances where the supplier is the obvious cause of performance problems and should take responsibility for the consequences.

The explicit definition of user obligations can help to avoid problems arising from user actions (or inactions). These often cover apparently 'common sense' assumptions that can later become a legal loophole. It may seem obvious, say, that a supplier should check that a site is suitable for a system. If something goes wrong, however, the supplier could blame the user for giving inadequate information, unless specific responsibilities have been spelt out. The specification of user responsibilities in the contract should alert management to the need to do something in the relevant activities.

FINANCING THE CHOSEN SOLUTION

A variety of financing options are available for financing and paying for IS facilities. For hardware systems, the basic choices are between outright purchase, rental or leasing. For other requirements, like software, the method of financing will depend on the nature of the product or service.

Obtaining Hardware

Purchasing a hardware system involves a one-off payment plus ongoing support, maintenance and insurance costs. *Rental* and some shorter-term *leasing* allows users to operate a system for the period of the contract, but without ever owning it; at the end of the contract the system goes back to the renter or lessor. Other leases, particularly longer-term ones, are a form of hire purchase, where a system is bought through the payment of the cost, plus interest, over a number of years. The system's manufacturer, an OEM, dealer or VAR may offer purchase and rental terms. There are also specialist companies who obtain systems from suppliers, then rent or lease them to users.

The key factors in deciding which approach to take include:

— the amount of cash available to an organisation or department;

— financial and administrative constraints on capital investment, as opposed to 'off balance sheet' *revenue expenditure*, such as rental and leasing costs;

— the likely payback period for a system or application;

— the likely rate of technological obsolescence and the ease with which new innovations can be introduced without disrupting operational new systems;

— the relative levels of tax relief obtainable on capital versus revenue expenditure;

— support levels available with different options;

— the amount of software, if any, included with different options;

— *total* costs of each option taking into account tax relief, interest payments, support, software, etc.

To Buy or Not to Buy

If an organisation or department has sufficient cash, buying a system is often the cheapest and best method. In some cases, however, there may be constraints on capital expenditure, even when the money is available.

There are two possible disadvantages with buying a system:

— Technological innovation may make it quickly obsolescent. This danger is less than it might seem in the fast-changing IT industry. A user invsts in a complete system and a total application, not just isolated pieces of hardware. So, even if the hardware is surpassed by a new development, the longer life cycle of the application will make switching to new hardware uneconomical, unless it is compatible with the installed system.

— Tax relief regulations may favour some forms of rental leasing over capital investments. For example, the 1984 Finance Act in the UK replaced 100% relief for capital expenses with 25% of the "written down" value at the end of each financial year. As computer prices fall so quickly, this greatly reduced the relief available on outright purchases. However, it still left 100% relief for rental and leasing, which are regarded as revenue expenditure. The current tax position for an organisation in relation to particular contracts must be carefully evaluated.

In many cases, these disadvantages will be relatively small compared to the extra costs involved in rental and leasing agreements and the small degree of extra flexibility they give for many systems.

The purchasing of a second-hand system could be an option worth considering. Second-hand computers are unlikely to prove to be technical 'duds', as in the second-hand car business, but they generally come with little or no maintenance and support. A second-hand system may be suitable if an organisation has the expertise and resources to support it adequately, or if the system is needed for non-essential tasks. The falling prices of new computers, however, can negate even the cost-advantage of a second-hand system: a brand new product with better capabilities may appear on the market at a similar, or lower, price.

Renting and Leasing

A wide variety of rental and leasing deals are offered by different suppliers. Rents are typically paid monthly on contracts that usually last for a year or less. Costs for rental are in general, significantly higher than list prices (and even higher than the discount prices at which rental companies usually obtain the system). The rental company should be expected to cover delivery and maintenance costs fully. The precise extent of such coverage must be defined in the contract. If any software is included, it should be explicitly mentioned.

Leasing falls into two basic categories: an *operating lease* and a *finance lease*. With an operating lease, the customer has rights only to use the system, not to own it. A finance lease, also known as *lease purchase*, enables a system to be bought over a number of years. Operating leases are usually shorter than finance ones — about three years compared to around five years.

In the competitive rental and leasing marketplace, many different facilities are offered to attract customers. For example, special terms may be provided to enable equipment to be upgraded. *Break* or *flex* points where equipment can be changed should be negotiated in most rental and leasing contracts, even for finance leases where the original system is, in theory, being bought. Whatever the facilities offered, expert advice must be taken when examining detailed contracts.

Paying for Software and Services

There was a time when systems software, like operating systems, was *bundled* inextricably into the price of hardware. Now, most software is generally *unbundled* and charged separately, even if only a nominal cost is made for some programs.

Packaged software is traded through *licences*. A licence can relate to a specific computer or to a specified number of systems on a network (known as a *site licence*). A one-off fee is usually paid for a licence, plus periodic service and other payments. The price, if any, of documentation and its updates must be agreed.

Charges for software updates should be carefully investigated. Software packages often have a number of major *releases* offering new and enhanced capabilities. Between new releases, there may be a number of *versions*, correcting bugs and making other improvements. Users can reasonably expect free and automatic receipt of new versions, at least, because they often include updates that bring capabilities originally promised. This should be clarified in the contract, as should the conditions under which a new release may warrant extra payments and a new licence.

Where software is tailor-made, the contract must state how costs are calculated, say on a fixed-price or time-and-materials basis. The ownership of such software must be clarified. If there is a possibility that it may subsequently be resold to third parties, the terms under which this is done should be specified, including the proportion of royalties the user will get.

In all software dealings, care must be also taken in identifying the performance criteria that have to be met before full payment can be expected — and what happens if the quality falls below acceptable standards.

Other services have their own cost criteria. For example, bureaux prices must be fully defined in terms of charges for machine time, storage space, communications capacity, installing links, carrying out any software or data coversion from existing systems, help-line support, etc. The cost calculations for other IS services, such as the use of consultants, maintenance companies and personnel agencies, should not be a problem, provided all potential charges are discussed and specified.

As with the overall contract, nothing should be left to chance or assumed implicitly in financing and cost negotiations. It is the best way of minimising the likelihood of receiving shocks from substantial 'hidden' costs.

External Sources of Funding

The general economic and social impact of IT has led to the growth of special support schemes from governments, international bodies (like the European Commission), industry associations and other sources.

Support may range from assistance in paying consultants to carry out feasibility studies, to grants covering implementation costs. Particularly innovatory applications may be assisted by funding designed to encourage research and development. Other help may be targeted at particular industries or applications. In addition, certain developments, particularly by smaller companies, may come under general business schemes. Regional or special development-zone assistance may also be applicable. All these kinds of alternative sources of funding should be investigated and considered.

SUMMARY: TYING UP THE LOOSE ENDS TIGHTLY

This chapter has emphasised the importance of treating the final phases of choosing a solution with as much thoroughness as other elements in the life cycle. Activities like evaluating responses to an invitation to tender and negotiating the contract are crucial to the ultimate success of a system, yet they are often hurried or neglected.

A number of common themes have been highlighted for making the final selection, negotiating contracts and finding optimum methods of financing the solution:

> *Keep business and user needs paramount.* The efforts taken during the feasibility study to understand and define applications requirements and cost/benefit guidelines will be undermined if they are not followed through in the final stages of system selection.

> *Analyse requirements systematically and comprehensively.* Careful thought and planning must go into preparing operational requirements, tender proposals, assessments, contracts and financing arrangements.

> *Be explicit and precise in specifying what is wanted.* Whether it is remembering human factors in operational specifications or clarifying legal contractual obligations, all relevant issues should be openly discussed at an early stage and resultant requirements explained unambiguously.

> *Have ambitious goals, but remain realistic.* The ultimate aim is to carry out extensive and complete investigations that will produce optimum solutions. In practice, however, there is rarely the time or resources available to do everything that would be theoretically desirable. All proposals and requirements should, therefore, be based on a realistic appraisal of what are the most important ingredients in creating successful IS solutions.

> *Don't underestimate human factors and software.* The roles of people and software are vital to determining the effectiveness of an information system. These issues are, however, the least tangible, and the most subtle and complex aspects of an information system. They must be given high priority during all phases of the IS life cycle.

10 Developing Systems and Software

MANAGING THE DEVELOPMENT LIFE CYCLE

The amount of in-house development needed for an application will vary greatly between projects. It may require an extensive software development effort lasting several years, or simply the relatively short-term task of bringing together a number of bought-in products. In all circumstances, the development must be undertaken with a systematic management approach, thorough planning and the effective deployment of competent IS professionals.

This chapter examines the key activities in the full development life cycle, with particular attention given to the overall management approach and the importance of applying formal engineering disciplines to software and system building.

The Main Development Activities

The development life cycle is, to some extent, a microcosm of the complete IS life discussed in Chapter 7. It starts with finding out user requirements and continues through analysis and designs to the production of working systems and subsequent maintenance and enhancement.

A variety of terminology is used to describe different development activities. They essentially boil down to the following main categories:

Analysis: finding out (*capturing*) user requirements, analysing them and producing overall requirements specifications;

Design: detailed models and specifications defining how the system is to be organised in terms of applications functions and technical capabilities;

Software implementation: program design, coding, testing and documentation;

Integration: bringing together all elements of a system to provide the final operational service;

Acceptance tests: ensuring the final system meets the requirements specification;

Operations: keeping live systems running effectively and efficiently;

Maintenance and enhancement: sorting out errors, upgrading facilities and adding new capabilities.

For simplicity, these functions may be depicted as following distinct sequential phases. In practice, they overlap considerably and boundaries between them are often fuzzy. There are two broad design categories: *functional* (or *top-level*) and *technical*. Functional designs overlap with requirements specifications in that they look at the system from the perception of the applications functions to be performed. Technical designs are concerned with detailed IS capabilities that support the functions.

Requirements analysis is sometimes known as *business analysis*. Many of the feasibility study activities discussed in Chapters 8 and 9 fulfil requirements capturing, analysis and specification needs.

Planning and Controlling Projects

In order to manage these development activities, projects must be well planned and their implementation monitored and controlled effectively. This involves:

— *estimating* project time-scales, costs, staff and other resource requirements;

— *planning* work in detail and being able to adapt the plan quickly and efficiently to take account of actual progress and changing requirements;

— *controlling and monitoring* progress on the development.

Estimation is vitally important, but difficult to get right. It must combine an effective theoretical model of how various factors interact, with the ability to include results and insights gained from practical experience. One of the first estimation models to gain widespread application was the *COnstructive COst MOdel* (*COCOMO*) developed by Dr Barry Boehm of TRW in the USA.

Models like COCOMO use estimating equations, based on descriptions of the project structure, development resources available and personnel attributes, to produce predictions of likely costs, schedules and staffing needs. The model should also be able to take account of factors like the required reliability of the developed software, the quality of development tools being applied, the skills of the professionals involved and the complexity of the final software. Once the initial estimates have been made, it should be possible to adjust them quickly to take account of actual performance and changing staff availability.

Estimates become the basis for detailed, phased plans which specify all activities that must be carried out, when and by whom. The higher levels in the planning structure are concerned with general management and reporting requirements, like allocating groups of tasks to individuals and teams. Regular reports must be received on work progress, co-ordinated by the team leaders who are responsible for ensuring all requirements are met for the detailed tasks under their control.

The completion of *timesheets* by project members is a common way of collecting information on progress. In addition, there are many computer-based *project management tools* that can assist with estimation, planning and control. The use of computers also helps to gather and monitor progress data automatically.

Imbalances in Life Cycle Costs

Without disciplined IS development management, serious imbalances occur in the distribution of effort and costs during the life cycle. Figure 10.1 illustrates roughly how the costs of software projects have tended to be distributed between the main development phases. While there has been some argument about the precise figures, the general proportions have been confirmed in many studies in the 1970s and 80s.

Maintenance consumes up to about 70% of project costs. A key reason for this is illustrated by Figure 10.2, which is based on research first carried out by Barry Boehm. It shows that the cost of fixing or changing software escalates dramatically in later life cycle activities. For example, it costs well over 100 times more to correct a bug during operation and maintenance than in, say, requirements analysis and design. Much of the maintenance costs, however, can be traced back to faults made in the initial designs.

The root cause of these problems has been the lack of a systematic approach to life cycle management. Poorly planned and structured

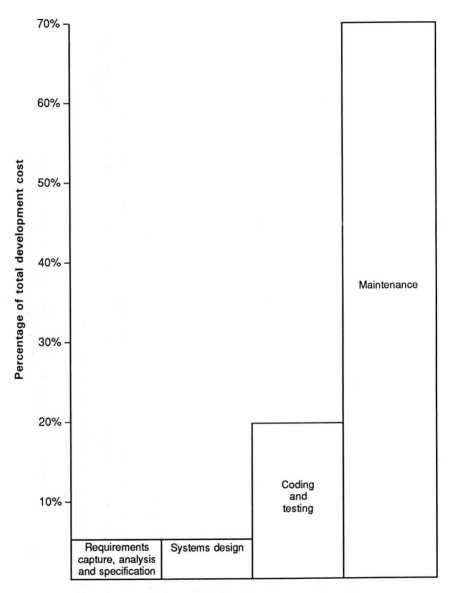

Figure 10.1   Distribution of Costs for a Typical Software Development Project

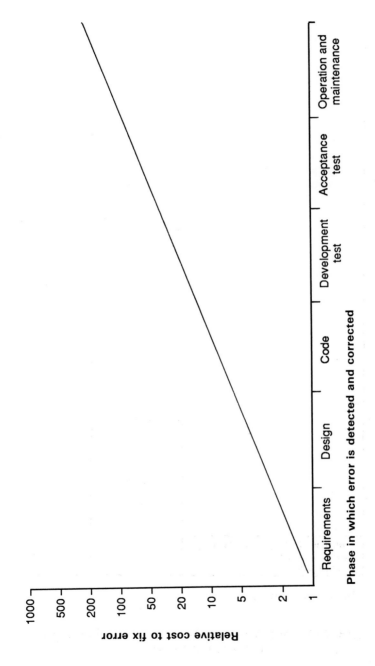

Figure 10.2 Cost to Fix or Change Software Throughout the IS Life Cycle

designs have led to unstructured program code that is difficult to unravel when changes must be made. Unravelling one knotty bug in the code can cause problems elsewhere. Adding new facilities is also error-prone because it means trying to integrate new code with the existing tangled web. Documentation is also often sparse and inaccurate, or non-existent.

At first, software development was seen almost entirely in terms of programming. Vast numbers of programs were written with minimal, if any, designs to guide them. In many cases, programming and design were virtually simultaneous activities. Clever, but complex, programming techniques may have been included to provide intellectual stimulation. Documentation of designs and programs has frequently been done hastily and inadequately towards the end of the project.

Over time, the situation has improved. Structured programming techniques have helped considerably to enhance the quality of coding. However, structured programs are truly effective only if they are derived from structured designs based on a precise and accurate understanding of user requirements. The success of a complete development depends on how the project is managed.

An awareness of the need for comprehensive structured IS development methods evolved gradually. Systematic engineering approaches began to be more generally used in the 1980s, but even then, only patchily. Even when most new projects use suitable engineering disciplines, there will still be many live operational systems based on approaches that are now regarded as unreliable and inefficient. Such systems will have to be maintained and enhanced for many years to come.

ENGINEERING SUCCESSFUL IS DEVELOPMENTS

The answer to the problems highlighted in Figures 10.1 and 10.2 is clear: spend more time in the earlier phases of diagnosing requirements, and getting an appropriate, resilient structural framework defined. Better-quality designs will lead to fewer errors in later stages. They will also mean that changes and additions can be made primarily at the design level, which is easier, more reliable and much less costly than doing them closer to the coding entrails.

The term *systems engineering* is used for the overall development. Within this, software engineering is the most problematical area.

Can Software be Engineered?

Developing software has many similarities to the building of physical constructions, like aeroplanes, bridges, office blocks and oil rigs. They all involve analysing requirements, producing detailed designs and integrating a variety of activities through effective project management techniques. They also all rely on a high level of technological skill, with individuals and teams often located at many sites. User and technical requirements can be extremely complex, involving the interaction of diverse factors. Time-scales are generally critical, with delays being very costly.

There are also many important differences. A key one is the fact that software developments lack established and proven engineering disciplines pertinent to the whole life cycle. The intangible nature of software is also an important unique characteristic which needs to be considered.

The construction of a physically-engineered product, like an aeroplane or house, consumes a substantial part of the development effort; the equivalent software production process of copying programs to suitable storage media is relatively trivial. Having a physical end-product also emphasises to the client or user that there should be a firm cut-off in specifying requirements.

Software, on the other hand, appears to be infinitely malleable. This frequently leads to what has been called *requirements creep*: clients and users wanting to try out slight variations and new ideas at all stages of the life cycle — and to carry on long after it has gone into live operation.

The amorphousness of software has also allowed many information systems to provide useful operational services, despite having many design flaws and program bugs. Most physical structures would collapse or teeter dangerously if they had been built with equivalent basic faults. Physical objects rarely have similar maintenance and enhancement difficulties as software.

Software engineering, therefore, must be based on its own special engineering concepts, techniques and implementation approaches. To be successful, software engineering must take account of the practical realities of software development, as well as seeking to meet theoretical goals of rigour and predictability common to other engineering disciplines.

Structured Development Management

There are three key ingredients in managing developments successfully:

— *methodologies*: systematic definitions of what must be done and when;

— *techniques*: how activities are carried out within a methodology;

— *tools*: the means used to carry out specific tasks.

All these aspects need to be structured in order to provide a sound framework on which developments can be built. Structured approaches include formal rules, notations and guidelines for creating specifications and designs.

The most lucid way of expressing such a structure is usually through a *design diagram*. For example, Figure 10.3 shows part of a diagram depicting the phases, tasks and activities in a management methodology. It is an *hierarchical* diagram: each element at a higher level can be the 'parent' to many 'children' in the level below, but each 'child' can have only one 'parent' with which it is associated. Many other structures and types of diagram are used, some of which are mentioned later in the chapter.

There are a number of concepts common to most design diagrams:

— Diagrams are composed of discrete units and interactions between them. The units may be known as *modules, objects, entities, items* or other terms appropriate to the specific diagram. Units are self-contained, with relationships between them defined through external interfaces.

— A design usually has multiple levels, starting at generic overviews and going down into greater detail. The process of breaking down the design into more detailed levels is known as *decomposition*, as in moving from phases to tasks to activities in Figure 10.3. This is known as *top-down* design because it starts at the highest level.

— The range of allowable relationships between elements in the structure varies between methodologies and techniques. For example, in an hierarchical structure, the only pathways are through the lines linking 'parents' and 'children'. Relational database management systems seek to provide maximum flexibility in permissible relations between data items.

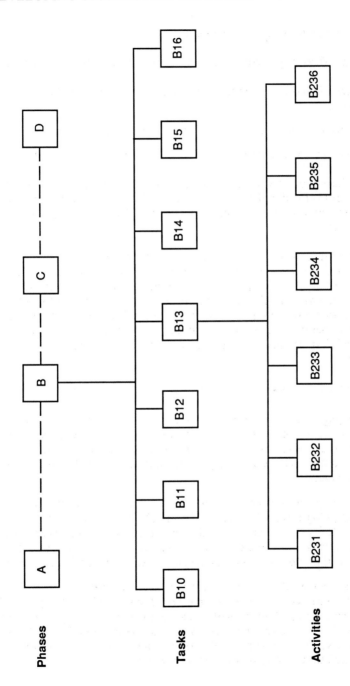

Figure 10.3 Example of an Hierarchical Structured Diagram

— The notations, rules and guidelines that govern design diagrams also vary between methodologies and techniques. For example, in Figure 10.3, the dotted line is an informal way of showing that there is a different relationship between each phase than between parent-child hierarchical lines. Precise definitions of design *symbols* (eg the boxes in Figure 10.3), relationship-connectors (eg full and dotted lines in Figure 10.3) and other specific conventions must be understood in order to make accurate sense of design diagrams.

Software Engineering Constraints

A number of methodologies, techniques and tools have been developed for discrete phases and tasks in the life cycle.

For example, structured programming techniques have been widely used since the 1970s, but they apply only to the coding phase of the life cycle. Various structured design techniques have been developed for earlier phases. Certain kinds of system, like real-time applications, have their own special design techniques. Formal techniques for requirements capture are taking longer to become established.

There are many inconsistencies and incompatibilities between these different techniques, which causes difficulties in moving between phases. Translating designs into software, for instance, can result in an error-prone and time-consuming process when there are different underlying concepts and conventions in the design and programming techniques used.

In order to be effective, structured techniques must be implemented *rigorously*. In many cases, however, their implementation has often been carried out only partially and without adequate discipline. Structured techniques adopted in theory have frequently been adhered to only informally in practice, thereby negating much of their value.

Computer-based aids help to maintain the necessary control in software developments. They can instil standards automatically, validate that formal requirements have been met and provide timely data on project progress. If designs are produced and maintained manually, checking them thoroughly is very time-consuming and difficult. In addition, many documents (sometimes known as *forms*) are created during developments: user interviews, designs, memos, etc. Computerised *forms management* is an efficient means of keeping track of all documents. The collection of project timesheet information from staff can also be performed more quickly and accurately using computers.

Until the mid-1980s, computer assistance was available primarily for programming tasks. Hence, there are many tools to help organise, develop and test programs. It was the growing availability of reasonably-priced graphical workstations and PCs that made it feasible to have widespread use of tools which can be applied efficiently to creating and manipulating design diagrams.

Although computer-aided software engineering (CASE) tools can help to improve software development control and productivity, their application does not guarantee success.

CREATING AN EFFECTIVE DEVELOPMENT ENVIRONMENT

On their own, even the best CASE tools cannot overcome basic management flaws. Automating the wrong approaches will still result in a wrong system, even if it is produced more quickly. Successful systems development depends on planning and co-ordinating methodologies, techniques and tools as a unified software engineering discipline.

The Development Strategy

A strategic plan is needed to define how projects are to be managed and run to meet corporate IS requirements. It must analyse the current environment and decide priorities for improvements. Guidelines for selecting methodologies, techniques and tools must be decided; development standards specified; budgets set; resource requirements planned; organisational structures, like projects, specified; and responsibilities allocated, including clear lines of command and reporting.

Like the coporate and IS strategies discussed earlier in the book, the development strategy must be regarded as an ongoing process, continuously adapting to lessons learned from experience and new requirements and technical innovations. Firm general objectives must be set to establish a framework for judging which approaches are acceptable.

In practice, an organisation may choose a number of different methodologies, to cater for the distinct characteristics of smaller projects compared to larger-scale developments. Systems based primarily on PCs and workstations for personal, rather than department or corporate applications, may need a special methodology. The imposition of a single methodology to cater for all needs could be cumbersome and counter-productive.

With structured techniques, the strategy should again be concerned with broad guidelines rather than specific details. It must take account of realistic, practical needs. The ultimate aim may be to achieve integrated coverage of the complete life cycle, but trying to do this quickly could create many technical and human problems, causing a massive retraining and relearning exercise. If staff have to get used to many new skills while trying to carry out important live developments, a great deal of anxiety can be caused, leading to a high level of errors and general inefficiency. If the new integrated approach is inappropriate for some aspects of the developments, it may be very difficult to make the necessary adjustments.

In some circumstances, such a transition to a totally new approach may be justified by the long-term benefits that can be achieved. In many organisations, however, a more suitable strategy will be to progress in an evolutionary way towards an integrated environment. The potential for interfacing with other techniques and tools should be an important criterion for any development innovations.

Methodologies and techniques define the context in which CASE tools are used. The tools must be capable of supporting appropriate structured approaches efficiently and reliably. It should always be borne in mind, however, that the choice of techniques to be used in the future could become constrained by the money and skills invested in particular tools.

The Case for CASE

It is ironic that software development has taken so long to make use of computer-based aids, when software has been applied to so many other work activities. Key reasons for this have already been outlined: the amorphous, complex nature of software; lack of agreed formal notations, standards and methodologies; and the relatively slow arrival on the market of tools to support development work.

In addition, there have been more human causes: the growth in computer applications, chronic shortages of skilled staff, and continuing maintenance problems with existing software have tended to focus IS management attention on 'getting things done' rather than establishing new approaches. Like many other people, software developers have been reluctant to abandon traditional skills and working practices in favour of new computer-based methods that could threaten the number of existing jobs and the relatively easy-going and satisfying conditions to which they have become accustomed.

CASE should, indeed, provide a more rigorous and closely monitored development environment. It will also drastically cut the need for certain job skills, particularly routine coding. On the other hand, a more effective management environment should make the work of software developers more efficient, not less interesting. There will also probably be a growth in demand for new CASE-based skills, such as in analysis, design and user support. The psychological resistance to CASE among IS professionals should be understood, but should not be allowed to prevent the introduction of any necessary CASE capabilities. This can be achieved by the same strategy as outlined in this book for other computer applications: consider *all* organisational, economic, human and technical issues systematically.

CASE is sometimes justified purely on the narrow economic grounds of 'improving productivity'. Of course, productivity must be a prime goal of CASE. But it is insufficient on its own. Producing designs or code more quickly can just create a 'faster disaster' unless it takes place within the right development environment. Efficiency is just one dimension that should be examined; other goals include:

— control of rigorous adherence to standards through automatic validation and verification of the techniques implemented;

— reliable and predictable development of consistent, high-quality designs;

— automation of routine and error-prone tasks, such as coding and documentation;

— enhancement of the job satisfaction of development staff by giving them the tools to do their work more effectively;

— support for project managers in co-ordinating and monitoring developments.

User Involvement in Developments

One of the main trends in systems development methods since the 1970s has been to try to give users simplified applications development tools which they can apply directly (as discussed in Chapter 2), such as:

— *applications generators*: which produce the required programs on the basis of information input by users in an easily understandable format, say by answering questions on a screen or filling in a form on a screen;

— *Fourth Generation Languages* (*4GLs*), which enable non-specialists to develop applications using a programming language that is easier to learn and manipulate than ones designed for IS professionals;

— *query languages*, such as SQL, and other easily-used means of accessing information in databases, rather than having to write programs to carry out the required searches and output presentation;

— *integrated development systems* which combine 4GL, query language, applications generation and database management facilities.

These 'end-user' applications development aids have an important role to play in the overall IS strategy. They enable some development workload to be moved away from systems professionals, whose time and skills can then be devoted to more complex technical needs. There are, however, some problems that can be caused by the use of 4GLs and similar tools. For example, 4GLs generally do not conform to structured software engineering standards and are less efficient in the use of machine resources than more specialist development tools. After all, user-oriented development approaches have been designed mainly to ease developments by non-specialists, rather than to meet the criteria expected by IS professionals.

Allowing users to develop 4GL-based applications without effective management co-ordination can also lead to a lot of wasted effort, with many users re-inventing the same applications. The involvement of users in systems development should, therefore, be carefully planned in the context of the overall IS strategy and specific software engineering policies.

DEVELOPMENT TASKS AND TOOLS

A wide variety of tools are available to support all the development activities outlined earlier in this chapter. They can be grouped into four categories:

— overall management co-ordination and control;

— analysis and design;

— database management, which overlaps with analysis and design, but has sufficient special requirements to make it worth considering separately;

— implementation, including programming, testing and maintenance.

Important elements that cut across all these activities are the *dictionaries* which contain information about designs, database structures and other objects and relationships relevant to different activities. CASE tools may have a design dictionary; database management systems (DBMSs) a data dictionary; operating systems a dictionary to help control various activities; and so on.

The information in dictionaries forms the basis of building and checking models that are needed to perform many life cycle tasks. Therefore, overcoming incompatibilities between dictionaries is crucial to establishing a consistent software engineering environment. This has led to much research and development into the concept of a unified *data repository* that could become the basis of an integrated CASE *software factory*. The repository would be the 'core' dictionary which provides consistent models that can be used by many different CASE tools, from a variety of suppliers, to carry out all development activities.

The data repository is a desirable long-term goal, although its implementation poses many practical problems, such as converting existing dictionaries into a form compatible with the new repository. The development strategy should, however, provide a staged, realistic plan for working towards such an *Integrated-CASE* (*I-CASE*) environment.

Managing with CASE

Managers of software projects typically have to produce desirable results from a situation involving:

— important, often critical, corporate and business goals;

— many users with varying needs;

— difficulties in knowing when user specifications are complete because of a continuous requirements creep;

— project teams consisting of many IS professionals whose skills are often in short supply;

— networked project environments where team members may be at different locations and may wish to work at different times;

— co-ordination of many different tasks which interrelate directly, or via shared database and directories;

— sophisticated data management capabilities;

— the complex assembly of program routines, modules, libraries and data which may be maintained in a number of versions during development;

— use of a variety of methodologies, techniques, tools and standards;

— rapid technological innovation.

Project management tools provide capabilities for estimating project costs and resources reliably; defining and adjusting plans; and gathering information on work done. They are based on structured approaches that help to instil systematic management disciplines.

The tools for planning and control are generally built on well-established techniques, like Critical Path Analysis and the Program Evaluation and Review Technique (PERT), which have been used successfully in many engineering projects since the 1950s. They represent sub-projects, activities and tasks that comprise a project as a diagrammatic network. These networks provide the framework for analysing and monitoring key aspects of a project, like the time and resources allocated to each activity, dependencies between them and the start/end dates for each task.

Estimation tools incorporate techniques like COCOMO to provide basic inputs to the planning process. Ideally, an integrated set of project management tools should be used to cover all project management needs:

Integrated Project Support Environments (IPSEs) aim to overcome incompatibilities between CASE tools and help manage and administer developments. IPSEs assist tools to interface with each other across the complete life cycle, within a consistent user/system interface. (They should not be confused with integrated program support environments that are targeted solely at the software production phase of the cycle, and which can also be abbreviated to IPSE.)

Open IPSEs allow for more flexibility in the choice of tools and techniques than closed IPSEs, which make it difficult and costly to introduce tools other than those predetermined by the IPSE supplier. The integration of tools into an IPSE should be simple and efficient in order to gain full benefits from any tailoring capabilities.

Configuration management is an important element in life cycle development support. It is needed to ensure the overall system remains coherent and consistent despite the many changes that must be made to individual parts of it during development and maintenance. For example, at any one time there may be many different versions of the same program module in existence, ie in live operation, acceptance testing and development phases. When a software system is being assembled for a specific application or product, effective configuration management ensures that all the right components, in their appropriate versions, are incorporated. The choice of configuration management tools and techniques should be considered as an important aspect of the development strategy.

Software quality management, as discussed in Chapter 7, must also be given high priority in the management of software developments.

Analysing and Designing Systems

Systems analysis and design in the front-end of the development life cycle consists essentially of:

— finding out what needs to be done;

— analysing requirements systematically;

— producing theoretical models which define in detail the processes, data and interactions involved in the required system;

— specifying the practical technical system that can be used to implement models.

Requirements capture is usually carried out relatively informally, through interviewing users, managers, etc and producing narrative reports, but there are some formal notations that can be used for capturing requirements directly in structured diagrammatic forms.

Structured diagrams are usually the most effective basis for most analysis and design tasks. Some of their basic principles were discussed earlier in the chapter and illustrated in Figure 10.3. They are generally preferable to text-based specifications because they show structures, objects and interrelationships in an easily understood visual format.

Design diagrams are used for all aspects of a system, from *enterprise models* of overall organisation and business needs to the most detailed elements of processes to be performed and data to be used.

Many different analysis and design techniques are available.There are general structured design approaches that can be used for most systems; and ones oriented to special types of applications, like the ultra-high reliability real-time systems demanded in defence and aerospace projects. Specialised techniques may also be needed for specific design tasks such as *data analysis*, which identifies theoretical requirements for data entities, attributes and relationships, independent of any particular DBMS. *Data flow diagrams* show relationships between data, processes and external factors, like customers. The term *object-oriented* design is used for techniques where the entities such as basic processes or data structures, relate to a complete object that is meaningful in the context of an application; *orders*, *invoices* and *products* are just such 'objects'. Other techniques break down designs into discrete elements that are less meaningful from the user's perspective. *Object-oriented programming* is the equivalent coding approach.

The long time taken to produce designs has been a major development problem. When a system is eventually completed, it may already be out of date because user needs have altered since requirements capture took place. Altering the system to meet changing needs has also often been too slow to keep pace with real-world dynamics.

Prototyping is a technique aimed at speeding up the process of developing designs. It enables a 'rough' design to be created quickly, which can be tried out by users to get a feel of how it will work. User reactions can be incorporated in a short time to produce an upgraded design. The design evolves through many of these steps, with close user interaction.

Analyst workbenches provide a co-ordinated means of carrying out most, or all, analysis and design from a single workstation. Key features of analyst workbenches should be the ability to:

— support appropriate methodologies and techniques;

— create and manipulate design diagrams directly;

— automatically check adherence to design standards;

— automatically verify that designs are consistent and unambiguous, using a design dictionary that co-ordinates the naming and use of objects, validity of relationships and other requirements;

— support prototyping approaches;

— help to produce documentation, which may involve substantial amounts of text as well as graphics;

— help manage and trace all design actions and forms.

Analyst workbenches are an important example of front-end (or *upper*) CASE tools.

Dealing with Databases

A DBMS is an important development and operational tool for the many information systems that involve the use of a database. A DBMS helps to structure information in the database. It is a vital bridge between theoretical data designs and working systems. Many fourth-generation application development tools are closely related to particular types of DBMS, such as relational systems.

The earliest DBMS structures were hierarchical (as in Figure 10.3) and *networked* (where each data item can have more than one 'parent' and movement between items can be in any direction). As discussed in Chapter 2, these approaches impose constraints on permitted pathways: fixed, top-downwards in hierarchical DBMSs and through pre-defined schema in network structures. Relational DBMSs (RDBMSs) offer greater flexibility because they allow relations to be created between any data items at the time they are needed to run an application.

The design of a RDBMS is concerned essentially with the definition of its basic two-dimensional tables, through a process called *normalisation*. This decomposes the overall mass of data into detailed tables. The relational model is most effective when there are many small tables. However, this creates efficiency problems at run-time because the complexity of relationships between data items increases as the number of tables grows. The performance of a RDBMS in carrying out its functions is, therefore, an important assessment criterion.

DBMSs tend to be used in two basic ways: to answer questions, and carry out transactions. Capabilities should be evaluated for both, because they are fundamentally different modes of action. Query systems leave the database unchanged. Transaction Processing (TP) applications can alter or delete data, so *integrity* checks must be made to see that information remains consistent during, and after, such amendments.

Data integrity controls ensure that a customer file is not deleted while there are still orders related to it, or that an order is not added without a valid customer reference. In online TP systems, such as booking services, integrity checks guarantee that all users accessing the database, often simultaneously, receive consistent information and are prevented from carrying out incorrect functions, like double-booking a seat or overwriting another booking.

Entity Relation (*ER*) DBMSs are a development of the relational approach which organise and manage many objects other than data. In CASE tools, for instance, an ER database can be used to handle user interview forms, data flow diagrams, program code, user manuals and other design entities.

Implementing Designs

The 'back-end' of the development life cycle consists of a number of crucial activities:

— detailed program design;

— program coding;

— Verification, Validation and Testing (*VV&T*) of programs;

— integration;

— acceptance testing;

— maintenance and enhancement;

— documentation of the completed system.

Structured programming techniques should be employed wherever possible as part of the general software engineering approach. As already discussed, there may be arguments in favour of end-user applications development tools that produce unstructured programs, but this should be done only if there are clear advantages that cannot be achieved in other ways and 4GL (or similar) developments are carefully co-ordinated and controlled within the overall strategy.

There are currently vast numbers of working systems that are based on poorly structured and documented software. *Reverse engineering* techniques have been developed to help unscramble the code of such software by creating structured programs and documentation from existing code. This assists the future maintenance and enhancement of the programs. Some back-end (or *lower*) CASE tools can generate structured code directly from designs. Interfaces between analyst workbenches and code generators can, therefore, make substantial contributions to development quality and productivity.

VV&T is initially applied to modules and subsystems. Verification checks the correctness of designs and code. Validation ensures required standards and formats are adhered to. The overall test program must also evaluate the user interface, performance, reliability and other criteria in the operational requirements specification.

Eventually, all elements in the system need to be integrated and final acceptance tests carried out. Even if individual subsystems have passed their tests, problems may be introduced when they are put together. Acceptance tests must ensure the complete system operates as it is expected to.

The amount of effort spent in maintenance and enhancement depends on the success achieved in earlier phases. If it involves delving into the innards of tangled code without the aid of adequate documentation, this activity will continue to consume a disproportionate share of resources, as shown in Figure 10.1. Good documentation is, therefore, important in all aspects of the development life cycle. Well-structured designs and code can be maintained properly only if they are fully and accurately documented. CASE tools assist the production and maintenance of documentation during analysis, design, programming, maintenance and enhancement activities.

SUMMARY: A STRATEGY FOR IS DEVELOPMENT

This chapter has examined key issues that must be considered in organising and managing systems developments. It has explained some of the special characteristics of software engineering which make it necessary for managers to ensure a disciplined approach is taken, from start to finish of developments.

The development strategy must be integrated with the overall IS strategy. It should:

— take a comprehensive balanced view of all life cycle activities;

— support systematic approaches to the planning and control of projects;

— aim towards an integrated set of methodologies, techniques and tools for all development activities;

— be realistic in providing phased plans for the transition from existing development environments to a new, more integrated and structured one;
— give priority to front-end analysis and design activities because this will substantially cut subsequent costs and resource commitment;

— establish and maintain rigorous software engineering disciplines, using CASE tools wherever possible to check automatically that standards are being followed;

— justify CASE investments on the basis of broad criteria other than just economic grounds, such as the motivation of IS professionals and technical requirements;

— take advantage of 4GLs and other end user tools in a controlled way that reaps the benefits of this type of approach while limiting their disadvantages;

— recognise that effective software engineering can contribute significantly to the ultimate success of information systems in meeting business goals.

11 Introducing a New Information System

PLANNING THE TRANSITION

The transition to a new IS service is a crucial phase in the life cycle, but is often neglected. It involves co-ordinating a large number of disparate issues, some of which may be forgotten or skimped in the rush to get a system up and running. Experiences during the transition can influence subsequent operations and attitudes for a long time. Any significant problems encountered can disrupt customer and client services, hamper production processes, lose orders, increase costs and create much anxiety among staff and managers affected by the system.

Failure to plan the transition thoroughly can also store up problems. For example, inadequate preparation of staff training and operational documentation will mean that the full benefits of the system are difficult to achieve. The transition should, therefore, be managed with as much systematic attention to overall goals and detailed requirements as would be paid to feasibility studies, systems development and live IS operations. An *implementation team*, reporting to the project manager, may be necessary to handle the transition on larger and more complex developments.

Key transition activities include:

— educating and training everyone affected;

— providing appropriate documentation for all users and activities;

— ensuring a suitable physical environment is provided for new hardware;

— converting data from previous paper-based or computerised formats;

— assembling the system in the working environment;

— acceptance testing and implementation;

— protecting the system from accidental, illegal or other unwarranted abuse;

— insurance of the system;

— consideration of legal aspects.

This chapter gives an overview of the tasks that need to be carried out in these areas.

PREPARING THE PEOPLE AFFECTED

A new information system can have a variety of direct and indirect impacts on many different groups and individuals, inside and outside the organisation. The people affected fall into three main categories:

— regular users who operate the system directly as part of their everyday routines;

— *casual* users who need to operate the system only intermittently;

— people who are affected by the system without being direct users.

The implementation plan should include systematic programmes of education, training, documentation and other support to prepare all these groups for what they need to know about the system.

Awareness of the Implementation Plan

All relevant user managers, professionals and staff must be forewarned about the internal implementation plan. If the joint project management approach recommended earlier in the book has been followed, there will be a formal mechanism where the views of all groups directly affected can influence the nature and contents of the plan. But even if, say, a departmental representative is on the project team, it does not automatically follow that everyone in that department is aware of the detailed plans. Leaflets, formal and informal meetings, newsletters and other techniques should be used to inform all levels in the company about the system's objectives and implementation schedules. An opportunity should be given for people to comment on the implementation plan and for that feedback to be taken into account by the project and/or implementation team responsible.

Early warning of potential practical problems is invaluable in making the transition as smooth as possible. If, say, physical alterations are proposed for an office at a time when the people working in it are likely to be under intense pressure, the transition could be eased if the schedule is altered accordingly. This will avoid the new system being perceived as an unwanted burden at a time when people have other key priorities; and it will demonstrate a practical response to local user needs.

The aim of IS awareness campaigns should also be to give a general understanding of the system, how it changes previous ways of doing things and why the new approach should be better. These awareness campaigns should also apply to relevant groups outside the organisation as some people external to the organisation may be regular users, such as travel agents linked online to a holiday tour operator. Others may be casual users, for example, bank customers with access to Automatic Teller Machines. And some may be affected in important indirect ways through changes to the quality of the services offered, such as a new form of billing or means of finding out information. All should be given appropriate information about the IS changes that apply to them.

Many IS projects have got off to a bad start, despite the improvements they provide, because insufficient attention has been given to telling people about why they are being introduced. Project teams often get so close to the system and its capabilities that they forget its benefits may not be self-evident to others. Even the best new systems often remove a capability that some people liked in the previous system. Explaining the rationale behind innovations can help to allay fears about impending changes and heighten the impact of attractive new features.

Pre-Installation Education and Training

The importance of continuing IS education and training has been frequently emphasised throughout this book, with a detailed discussion in Chapter 5. Although much valuable learning can take place only after practical experience has been gained of live operations, education and training in the pre-installation period is equally important. It helps build confidence and remove anxieties, which enables benefits to be gained more quickly and extensively than if users have to go through a long learning curve.

The type of education and training given must be tailored to the needs of each type of user: regular or casual, internal or external. An important pre-installation activity can be the retraining of managers and staff who have to be redeployed because of the new system, or who have to learn new skills to exploit changes in their computer-assisted working methods.

IS education and training is an integral part of preparing the whole organisation for the diverse impacts of IT. A new IS service can change job descriptions in a variety of ways, as well as eliminating some jobs and creating totally new ones. Concern about these changes often underlies management and staff resistance to the introduction of new systems. Appropriate education and training is a prime means of ameliorating these negative attitudes and ensuring the ability and skills of all employees are deployed in the most effective way.

IS professionals should be made aware of developments they are not working on personally. The introduction of CASE-based environments and tools can also require substantial preparation of all development staff before new systems are introduced.

The design of user/system interfaces (see Chapter 9) has a strong influence on determining the amount of direct operational training that has to be provided. Systems that are difficult to understand and manipulate require much more pre-installation effort than ones which are genuinely easy to use.

Providing Appropriate Documentation

The need for good documentation is another priority that has been reiterated throughout this book. Documentation needs must be considered and dealt with systematically from the start of a project because it is often much harder and more expensive to overcome problems at a later stage.

The term 'documentation' has become misleading because much information that was once on paper can now be built into the system, through computer-based systems using on-screen messages and other interactions that guide users automatically through the system. In the following discussion, 'documentation' should be taken to include non-paper media. The quality of user/system interactions is again important, for example, to ensure clear information appears on the screen which allows users to carry on with an operation without reference to a printed manual.

The audience aimed at by particular documentation elements should be analysed and specified for three main purposes:

— introductory information to give an overview of the topic involved;

— educational material that helps to instruct actual users;

— reference information needed to solve problems and advise users during live operation.

These requirements can be satisfied in a variety of forms: marketing leaflets, booklets, manuals, newsletters, user notices and built-in user/system interactions. The appropriateness of a system's document-ation can be judged according to criteria such as:

— having as much information as possible integrated into the system through menus, dialogues, help screens, etc;

— clarity in defining the target audience and ensuring any jargon used will be understood;

— being able to present information in a manner tailored to a specific application or user, which may mean integrating information from a supplier with the organisation's own application-specific documentation;

— effectiveness of educational material in imparting the information and skills it is supposed to;

— speed and precision with which access can be made to reference information that may be needed only occasionally, for example, when something has gone wrong;

— provision of basic 'start-up' information that guides novice users with step-by-step instructions to start a system;

— availability of 'wind-down' instructions which explain what to do to finish a task, close-down an online session or switch off a computer;

— having effective, efficient support, including a convenient and timely updating service.

Full details of the documentation to be provided, and how and when it is to be updated, must be specified in the contract.

Marketing the IS Service to Users

The introduction of a new system offers an opportunity to market its benefits to users, in the way that a commercial service is sold to its potential audience. In some instances, the new system will be the basis of a new service or product that will be the subject of its own marketing campaign anyway, but consideration should also be given to marketing the IS service in its own right.

Even if user departments within the enterprise have been involved in the project team, significant benefits can be gained from promoting the service when it is introduced. It will ensure that everyone is alerted to the introduction and they understand what it aims to achieve. If it is well marketed, more positive attitudes will be created towards it. For example, the new system could be given a name and identifying image of its own. The introduction could be linked to launch competitions, brochures and any other activities associated with the launch of a new product or service.

After the initial bout of publicity, further marketing initiatives should be undertaken on a continuing basis, eg when significant changes are made in upgrading the service. Marketing aids can also be used to get feedback from users on how they view the system and to provide information, say through regular newsletters.

Many of the functions performed under this marketing umbrella could be seen as part of other responsibilities, like education and user support. Perceiving it as a marketing exercise, however, can give it a sharper focus and more bite, because it will be tackled as a pro-active selling task rather than a more re-active, passive requirement.

SYSTEMS MIGRATION

Unless an organisation or application is being started totally from scratch, a migration path must be planned from the existing information system to the new one. This may mean moving from a largely manual system to a computer-based approach for the first time; or it may involve going from one set of hardware and software to another.

Migration plans cover the scheduling of a variety of activities, from preparing the physical environment, through systems conversions to final system assembly and acceptance testing. For some projects, it will make sense to put one person, or a team, in charge of co-ordinating migration. Responsibilities for specific activities, like software conversion or hardware installation, will still remain with the relevant functional unit.

Creating a Suitable Working Environment

Many computer systems can now, in theory, operate in any ordinary working environment. However, problems can be caused if insufficient care is taken to ensure that there are adequate physical amenities for a particular mix of systems, people and activities. This demands consideration of a wide spectrum of factors:

Space. Sufficient space must be provided to enable the installation to be configured for optimum work efficiency and user comfort. The requirements of ancillary equipment, such as cabling and power supplies, should be considered, in addition to the system's prime hardware units.

Room climate. Air conditioning, humidity regulators and other environmental controls may be needed, for example to cope with the heat generated by computers.

Lighting. Room illumination must be geared to the operation of equipment which itself emits light, such as PCs or VDUs. It should be possible to site equipment in relation to natural and artificial light sources to minimise glare and reflections.

Noise. Some computer equipment, particularly printers, can cause a great deal of noise. In the interests of human health and working effectiveness, noise generated by computer-based systems should be kept to no more than about 5dB(A) above background levels, except for high pitched feedback signals for warning purposes (the noise-measuring unit *dB(A)* indicates the level of human perceptions of sounds in decibels, *dBs*). In some circumstances, *acoustic hoods* may be needed to dampen the noise of printers; these hoods can cost a significant amount, particularly if an organisation has many printers, and can sometimes cause operational problems, such as printer heating.

Room furnishing. Curtains, venetian blinds, carpets and other room fittings and decorations should be given careful consideration to ensure they take account of any special needs. For example, floor covering should be made of anti-static material because computer systems generate a great deal of static electricity; and curtain, wall and ceiling colours and surface textures should seek to give optimum levels of light reflectance.

Power points. There should be sufficient suitable power points to permit flexibility in positioning equipment.

Cabling. Computer systems can involve a great deal of cabling. Wherever possible, cabling should be hidden for safety reasons, which may mean having to provide false ceilings and floors.

Storage areas. Space will have to be set aside for storing disks, tapes, stationery supplies and other necessary support items. These may need special security and environmental controls, say for disks and tapes containing back-up information.

Facilities for specialist IS activities. Accommodation will obviously be needed for specialist in-house IS professionals. In larger installations, special operator rest rooms may be necessary; access may be needed to them outside normal office hours if multi-shift operation is required, which may also lead to the need for canteen services. Accommodation may also have to be provided for external consultants and on-site engineers.

Security and safety. Requirements for equipment protection, fire safety and other security controls must be considered in selecting sites and preparing the environment (see *Vulnerability and Security* later in this chapter).

Contracts with suppliers should clearly indicate how responsibility for preparing the environment should be shared. Suppliers of some hardware may be expected to inspect conditions beforehand, so they can advise on what alterations should be carried out. The task of preparing the environment may be contracted to an external supplier if there are insufficient in-house resources or expertise.

Converting Data for the New System

Converting data from the existing system can be a major and time-consuming effort. The process must be scheduled to ensure live operation is not held up because the conversion is delayed. Extra staff should be employed to cope with the peak conversion workload, if necessary. For example, conversion from a manual system could demand a major clerical effort. Some existing information may be in computer-readable form, but much paper-based data will have to be converted by being keyed-in from workstations.

Converting from one computerised data format to another has both hardware and software dimensions. At a physical level, the nature of the storage medium may have to be changed, say from tape to disk or from one type or size of disk to another. Software has to have data presented to it with particular codes and formats, so existing data may be incompatible with new software even if it is held on an appropriate hardware storage medium. There are many automated aids that can assist in this conversion, particularly where widely used protocols and products are involved. A significant amount of special development work may be needed, however, to carry out the translation of information from one computer system to another.

The use of a DBMS poses significant conversion problems, whether moving from unstructured files to a DBMS for the first time, or from one structure to another. These are such complex issues that they can be addressed only as part of the prime development effort. The phasing of detailed conversions, however, could come within the remit of the special team co-ordinating implementation.

Data conversion provides an opportunity to 'clean up' files. Once the information to be converted has been identified, an attempt should be made to check its accuracy. A useful technique for doing this is to show it to the people to whom it refers: customers, suppliers, staff, etc. In addition to ensuring the data is correct, this can be used as a means of engaging the people affected in discussion and consultation about the new system.

Assembling the New System for Implementation

A new information system could consist of many different elements, from a variety of sources, such as:

— computer processors;

— workstations and terminals;

— data storage media;

— printers and acoustic hoods;

— telecommunications lines and control equipment;

— network controllers;

— cabling;

— stationery, printer ribbons, etc;

— decollators, bursters and guillotines for stationery;

— air conditioning and environmental controls;

— furniture and fittings;

— special *uninterruptible power supplies* to maintain consistent electrical supplies;

— shelving and other storage equipment for disks and tapes;

— *stand-by generators* to take over if the main source of electricity is broken off;

— systems software;

— applications software.

The myriad activities that can be involved in administering and checking the co-ordinated delivery of all these items can be a major task in itself. Some of these items may be coming directly from an outside supplier; the source of others may be within the organisation. Deliveries should be phased to ensure they occur in the right sequence and to avoid suppliers stumbling over each other trying to install different equipment at the same time.

Hardware being migrated from one location to another has to be decommissioned and recommissioned correctly by experts. Software licences may have to be changed because programs are being moved to processors or sites not covered by the original licence. Transportation of equipment between internal sites must be carefully planned. Explicit responsibilities must be allocated for each task in the assembling process, otherwise they may be forgotten. For example, someone should be in charge of accepting all deliveries and forwarding them to the appropriate location. In many cases, equipment has been mislaid because it has been put in a corner and forgotten after delivery. A special implementation help desk can help to cope with the peak growth in queries and problems that is likely to arise during the implementation of systems involving substantial changes to previous working environments.

Acceptance Testing and Implementation

Testing takes place at many stages in the selection and development of systems. As discussed in Chapter 9, benchmark and other tests are important aids to evaluating systems. Systematic testing is also an integral part of the development life cycle.

Acceptance tests need to be carried out in the environment where systems will run live applications. They must check the performance of individual elements, such as major hardware units, as well as the system as a whole, once it has been fully assembled. Bugs sorted out during acceptance tests will help to make migration to the final service smoother and quicker. Pressure to bypass or shortcut acceptance testing to bring forward live operation should, therefore, be resisted.

The changeover to live running will vary considerably in complexity, length and cost. For a smaller self-contained application, it can happen virtually overnight. In other circumstances, it may be necessary to have a period of *parallel* running, in which the old and new system exist side by side until there is sufficient confidence to make the final transition.

Parallel operation has many drawbacks. It can cost a lot and require much extra staffing. It can also permit some staff to cling to old habits and ways of working. In addition, the support provided by the old system may disguise some weaknesses in the new service which will become apparent only after the switch-over to total live operation has been completed.

Parallel running should be employed only when it is essential, and for the minimum period that makes sense. Phased, step-by-step introductions, including *pilot projects* if necessary, should be given strong consideration as an alternative means of maintaining stability during transition and implementation.

Pilot projects are usually targeted at a subset of the overall system, such as a limited number of users or only one application area. They can be used for live operations or in simulations that mimic an actual working environment. A pilot should never be seen as an isolated experiment, but as an intrinsic part of the overall development process. Results from it should be thoroughly evaluated and the lessons learnt transferred systematically to help the full implementation of the final service.

A phased introduction of different aspects of a system helps to minimise the risk of teething problems turning into something far worse. The first applications implemented, or pilot projects, should be relatively self-contained, so that problems encountered can be isolated, without causing broad organisational or business disruptions. They should also demonstrate that tangible and substantial benefits can be gained to convince users that the system offers meaningful advantages to them.

Once the new system has been satisfactorily tested and put into full live operation, the work of the implementation team will be over and its members can move to other activities.

VULNERABILITY AND SECURITY

A computer-based information system is a valuable resource. It can be vital to continuing organisational operations. Information contained within it can be of enormous social, personal, commercial, political, national and international importance. Therefore, any disruption to an IS service may have serious consequences. Illegal or unwarranted access to information can be used to the detriment of the people and enterprises concerned. Monetary theft can take place purely through the manipulation of an IS service.

Regular *risk assessments* should be carried out to evaluate areas of vulnerability. These should be conducted with the assistance of experts in security, disaster recovery, insurance and other relevant disciplines.

Physical Controls

Some important items of hardware, like floppy disks and personal computers, are vulnerable to direct theft. Other hardware could be used illegally *in situ* if someone gains access to the room where it is kept. Accidental or deliberate damage to hardware can also prove costly and cause severe operational problems. Physical access to rooms containing hardware should be subject to appropriate checks, ranging from special security devices, like entry-card and voice-recognition systems, to the general controls that apply to anyone coming into an office block.

As with any security system, a balance must be maintained between allowing normal work to continue efficiently and providing effective safeguards. Distinctions must be made between different levels of vulnerability, so that the more valuable systems are given a higher degree of cover. For example, a data centre containing basic IS infrastructure systems and large amounts of sensitive corporate information should have strict security controls. Only authorised personnel should be allowed access to the building and priority should be given to having good quality security and hazard protection. The site of the data centre should be chosen to aid security control and the building itself should not be easily recognisable as a computer centre.

With an office information system, however, less rigid precautions may be needed. Secure cupboards and other storage facilities should be provided for storing floppy disks and other data storage devices, as they should for any valuable items. Otherwise, sensible general measures should be adequate, such as locks on doors, guards after normal working hours, water sprinklers and fire hydrants, flood barriers, etc.

Recovery Procedures

The aim of successful security and risk management is to lower the probability that something will go wrong. It can be prohibitively costly, or disruptive to acceptable working procedures to reduce that probability beyond a certain point — and virtually impossible to guarantee a completely risk-free environment. *Disaster-recovery* plans are, therefore, essential.

There is a natural tendency for people to cope with potential disasters by subconsciously believing it will never happen to them. Lip service may be paid to the need to guard against disasters, but in practice doing something about it becomes a low priority. This makes the potential cost of security controls, backup systems, etc, seem an unacceptable price to pay for something that, at worst, is perceived as a remote possibility. People who have experienced the damaging effects of fires, hurricanes, bombs, thefts and other mishaps realise how important an effective disaster-recovery plan can be; but by then it may be too late. This IS strategy should, therefore, include provision for:

— *data backup* capabilities and procedures;

— *standby* systems that can be switched into action in an emergency, such as generators for power supplies and specific items of hardware, or complete systems, onto which workloads can be moved quickly and smoothly;

— *recovery procedures* detailing what users and IS professionals must do to cope with a serious system disruption.

Having a plan is insufficient in itself. It must be regularly monitored and tested to see that it remains realistic and that people are aware of their responsibilities within it. Sound theoretical security systems often prove to be ineffective in a crisis because they have been poorly supported and maintained.

Although the term 'disaster recovery' sounds dramatic, many of the procedures involved are relatively mundane. For example, taking regular backup copies of data and storing them in a secure location should be part of everyday working practices. If this is done properly, recovering from the loss of current data files will be greatly eased.

Basic system design capabilities can also facilitate recovery procedures. For example, systems with a truly modular structure isolate faults within discrete units so that operations can continue, perhaps at reduced performance, while the fault is corrected (which is known as *graceful degradation*). If the system comes to *clean shut-down*, starting it up again will be more reliable because the consistency and integrity of the system will have remained intact. Comprehensive automatic logging of system activities can help re-establish the conditions when a break occurred by tracing the actions identified in the resultant *audit trail*.

Some IS service companies specialise in providing disaster recovery assistance, such as a standby installation or secure storage for backup and archived data.

Privacy and Data Protection

Computer-based information systems take the potential for information abuse onto a different scale than is possible with paper files. Of course, information on paper can be stolen or looked at without permission. An online database, however, is designed to allow much more information to be accessed efficiently at one time; the *raison d'être* of an online DBMS is to enable data gathered in one place to be shared by many users, at many locations. Concern that this could lead to a serious invasion of privacy has caused many countries to introduce *data protection* laws specifying the rules under which information can be gathered, stored and used, particularly with computer systems.

In the UK, for instance, the Data Protection Act of 1984 covered most personal data held on computers, but not paper-based information. Exceptions were made for specific types of databases, such as those used in payroll systems and the prevention or detection of crime. It set up a *Data Registrar* to establish and maintain a register of *data users* and computer bureaux holding personal information on computers.

A number of basic principles were specified in the Act for registered data, such as that it is: obtained fairly and lawfully; held only for specific and lawful purposes; not be used or disclosed in a manner incompatible with the purposes specified when registering; accurate; kept up to date; and stored for no longer than is necessary. *Data subjects*, the individuals to whom the personal data relates, have a right to know, on the payment of a fee, what information is stored about them; how it was gathered and used; and to whom it will be disclosed.

Every organisation holding computerised data must carefully consider the requirements of this kind of legislation. Costs and technical facilities needed to implement such provisions, like providing data subjects with accurate and full information, should be taken into account during feasibility studies.

Many countries have similar legislation, perhaps with different detailed obligations and rights; but some countries have no specific data protection laws. Organisations should be aware of the data protection legislation applicable in each country in which they operate.

Investigations must also be made into any guidelines or laws relating to the movement of computerised information between countries, sometimes known as *transnational data flows*. In addition to data protection laws which affect the transfer of files between countries, other relevant factors include customs regulations, trade tariffs, and policies aimed at protecting and exploiting national 'information resources'.

International bodies like the Organisation for Economic Co-operation and Development (OECD) and the Council of Europe have developed guidelines on transnational data flows aimed at promoting greater consistency in all countries. Implementing such guidelines, however, poses immense practical and political problems. For instance, it is difficult to monitor digital information to check its contents, say to see if it consists of a traded 'product', without instituting unacceptable levels of regulated supervision of all communications. Transnational data flow regulations or proposals are agreed or amended from time to time. Organisations involved in international dealings should keep in touch with such developments.

Protecting Access to Information Systems

Having legislation to protect privacy on computer databases is meaningful only if there are mechanisms for preventing unauthorised access to information in them. Checks are also needed to guard against criminal acts, such as illegal tapping into computer networks (called *hacking*). These controls must be built into the basic operational mechanism of a system. For example, checks should be made on the *password* supplied by each person trying to gain access from a workstation to an online database or network. Each user should be associated with a particular set of authorisation levels determining what that person is allowed to do in the system. Checks can also be made on what tasks are permitted from workstations in certain locations.

In order to implement these constraints, various *locks* and controls must be built into the system. For example, a DBMS should lock out users who lack the appropriate *key* to access an item of information in prescribed ways (such as being able to read but not update the information); keys are allocated in association with passwords.

An audit trail should automatically track all activities and transactions in the system to enable any unwarranted use to be traced to its source; so for example, it should be possible to find out who carried out a particular transaction, when, and from what location.

The control mechanism used can itself be a source of vulnerability to those with sufficient expertise. Confidential data, like lists of passwords and related users, must be stored somewhere in the system if checks are to be made automatically. A high-level user, like an IS or Services Manager, needs to have legitimate access to update this type of information.

The existence of such sensitive directories and the ability to access them is one of the system's vulnerable points targeted by criminals. Expert hackers may be able to break into these files through ingenious routes, or someone can find out the authorised password that allows access. Special precautions must, therefore, be taken with such system files.

Computer Crime

There has been an inevitable growth in computer-related crime as the use of IT has grown. It is difficult to be precise about the extent of such crime because it is often difficult to detect — and when it has been discovered, companies are often reluctant to prosecute because it could expose the vulnerability of the service provided to customers and clients.

The crimes that sometimes get most publicity, often in fictionalised forms, are ones that involve great technical ingenuity. In the late 1980s, for instance, the notion of a computer *virus* became the focus of much coverage in the mass media. A virus is a program, introduced into software, which 'infects' other programs, for example causing them to delete key data files.

Many crimes are carried out without recourse to specialist IS knowhow, say by falsifying input or transactions. Users with approved access can deliberately misuse the system, although they follow the authorised procedures accepted by automated security checks. Of course, some crimes do require special IS expertise to execute. For example, a *trojan horse* is a routine embedded in an official program which performs an illegal or damaging operation when it is activated by some external event, like the computer's clock indicating a particular time or day of the month.

The security precautions discussed in this chapter can help to lessen the risk of computer crimes and increase the likelihood of misdemeanours being detected if they do occur. In addition, the nature of the overall management and working conditions can help to limit criminal opportunities and the personal grievances that often motivate employees to take illegal actions.

In the past, the idea for a computer crime has often come from operational failures and poor management control, which have accidentally shown that it is possible to 'get away with' something, like double payments for an order. Personal problems and dissatisfactions can also cause previously honest managers and staff to use their access to an information system to boost their income or take 'revenge' against a manager, or the organisation as a whole.

The IS management procedures described in this book are aimed at creating an environment in which the controls and attention to human needs should discourage computer crime.

INSURING THE SYSTEM

The value of an information system to an organisation and to individual users is usually far greater than the direct investment put into it. If a key IS service fails, many important operations can be seriously hampered or stopped. Adequate insurance cover must be provided for the *material damage* and *consequential loss* that can be caused to, and by, a computer-based system.

Material damage involves assessing the worth of individual items affected by fire, accidents, theft, sabotage, etc. For hardware, this is reasonably straightforward, as long as the policy covers all relevant items, such as power supplies, cables, air conditioning and other accessories and auxiliary equipment, in addition to the main computer systems. When it comes to software and data, material damage is a trickier issue. The face value of a physical data storage medium is often far less than the information stored on it. For instance, a cheap floppy disk could hold programs essential to a crucial commercial activity. Insurance cover, however, is likely to allow for only the cost of the medium, unless specific alternative provisions are made.

The consequential loss to the organisation of a serious disruption of information service, or loss of key software and data, can be extremely difficult to assess. It requires a thorough examination of the complicated sequence of events that may follow, affecting users, suppliers, customers, clients, other organisations and/or the general public.

The complexity and importance of consequential loss requirements mean that they should be sorted out in explicit detail at an early stage, before an incident occurs. Special insurance and legal experts should be consulted, as negotiations are likely to go beyond provisions contained in standard contracts. Damages for consequential loss frequently apply only after a defined period (for example, a breakdown of over 24 hours) and continue for a prescribed length of time. In addition, insurance contracts, either for material damage or consequential loss, often specify that appropriate security and safety precautions must be taken.

LEGAL ASPECTS

There are a number of laws which relate directly to computer-based systems, such as those covering data protection. Many traditional laws, however, have been found to be inadequate when applied to computer-based systems.

Software copyright, for instance, has been poorly served by traditional copyright laws. So, there have been amendments to old laws and special provisions in new legislation, such as in the 1988 Copyright, Designs and and Patents Bill in the UK. Software copyright may be an important issue if an organisation develops its own programs, perhaps as a joint project with an outside systems house, or if there is a copyright dispute over a bought-in package.

Legal problems can also arise in finding evidence that is admissible in a Court of Law. Information recorded directly by computer may be dismissed unless convincing proof is offered to show that the system is accurate and reliable. New computer-related categories of crime, like hacking, can be difficult to prosecute under legislation which fails to take account of electronic information techniques.

The use of computer-based library and information services, like teletext and viewdata, can pose possibly contentious legal questions about the nature of 'publishing' activities. For example, what proof can be provided if an alleged libel was seen by the complainant on only a workstation screen linked to an electronic 'publishing' service, but the information has subsequently been erased from the system? If the operation or malfunctioning of a computer system causes some damage to an individual or group, the question of legal liability could arise. As IT pervades even more business and social activities, the scope for such occurrences will increase.

During the preparation for a new system, it is not possible to identify all the legal aspects that will arise in the future. However, contacts must be made with experts to review the existing legal situation and establish continuing procedures for monitoring and handling subsequent developments.

SUMMARY: CO-ORDINATION START TO FINISH

This chapter has outlined the many factors that have to be co-ordinated during the final phases before a system goes live. The diversity of the issues involved and their importance to successful operations highlights the importance of managing them in a co-ordinated way, to a systematic plan.

The basic principles that should be incorporated in managing the transition and implementation include:

— allocation of specific responsibilities for co-ordinating detailed transition and implementation, perhaps through a special implementation team;

— high priority given to preparing, training and encouraging people affected to make optimum use of the system as quickly as possible after it is introduced;

— systematic attention to all practical details in preparing an appropriate working environment;

— careful scheduling of all tasks involved in migrating to the new system, with provision made for any extra resources needed for conversion effort, parallel running, etc;

— recognition that the assembling of constituent elements of a system may be an important responsibility in its own right within the project, including the co-ordination and acceptance of all deliveries;

— the introduction of a live system should be sensitively phased and preceded by adequate testing of the total system;

— the implementation should be integrated with the overall IS strategy to ensure that key aspects, involving significant costs, are taken into account from the earliest phases, such as insurance, accommodation and legal implications.

12   Providing an IS Service

SERVICE MANAGEMENT RESPONSIBILITIES

Once an information system goes live, it must continue to provide an effective service to users who rely on it to carry out their jobs. A *service management* function must be identified to take responsibility for this ongoing requirement.

The nature of the IS service management role depends on the size of the organisation and the systems involved. In smaller enterprises, it could be integrated with other IS responsibilities. In larger organisations, and with larger systems, a special IS Service Manager, with associated group or department, will probably be needed.

Service management could be primarily a centralised corporate function, particularly when operations are built around one or more data centres; in some cases, the title Data Centre Manager is synonymous with that of IS Service Manager. However, where there is a decentralised IS strategy, the corporate management team may be relatively small, with its prime concern being to co-ordinate the operations of distributed computing systems under the control of user management.

Service management activities include:

— technical development and support of the day-to-day operational service;

— servicing users' operational needs;

— site preparation and implementation;

— operational security control;

— administration of accessories and supplies.

External IS suppliers can undertake many of these activities.

Importance of the Service Function

The service function is at the sharp end of an IS department's contact with users. Problems that arise during systems development can often be overcome before the system goes live. Service difficulties, however, may become apparent to users immediately. Yet the development function is frequently given higher status and rewards than service management.

Despite the tendency to treat them as relatively unskilled staff, some operations specialists have a better understanding of actual user needs because they have to sort out problems that may have been caused by development failures. There is also much overlap between the technical skills involved in service and development activities. For instance, considerable software expertise is needed by data centre staff to tune the performance of systems software and carry out their own in-house software developments.

Opportunities should be provided for the movement of IS professionals between service and development functions. Service staff can be particularly effective in user support activities because of the expertise they gain in coping with a broad range of practical problems.

As with all IS specialists, service experts should be able to move out into business and corporate functions if they have the ability, while a technical career path should be available for those who wish to develop their IS skills.

Are Data Centres Necessary?

The establishment of special centres devoted to the operation of computer systems has many benefits for companies with workloads of sufficient size. They provide economies of scale in purchasing and running hardware and software. Once such a data centre has been established, the volume of transactions it handles can increase at relatively low incremental cost. The development and management of skilled service staff can also be more cost-effectively co-ordinated within these centres.

Data centre justifications are most obvious for large-scale batch and TP workloads. More than one data centre may be advisable for management and operational efficiency. In many circumstances, however, workload requirements and user needs may be best handled by operations that are more closely integrated with other user or IS activities. Decisions about whether to have a data centre, how many to have, how to structure the IS service function and other related issues must always be taken within the context defined by the corporate IS strategy (see Chapter 6).

MANAGING A DATA CENTRE

The choice of data centre location is important. In modern networked environments, there is no longer an intrinsic reason why it has to be close to business units, unless there are special input/output delivery requirements. The data centre could, therefore, be sited in areas of relatively low rents and land values. It should not, however, be too remote from urban areas where pools of skilled staff are likely to be found, particularly as it may be desirable to house development staff in the same building.

Security criteria should also influence the siting of data centres (see Chapter 11). For example, it should be possible to control access to the centre and make its appearance reasonably anonymous, to avoid attracting the attention of people who could want to harm it.

Telecommunications and networking will be an integral part of data centre activities. Strong co-ordination is needed between data centre and telecommunications managers to integrate their operations effectively. For instance, support teams should consist of professionals with a mix of skills and training and should recognise the overlaps in these activities.

Multiple data centres are most likely to be successful where the workload can be split cleanly into independent applications which can then be completed with little, if any, access to other centres. If lots of information has to be exchanged between centres, operations will become costly and complex. This negates the prime advantages of having data centres in the first place, which are to streamline operations and maximise the return gained from IS investments.

An organisation could choose to contract out the operation of data centres to a facilities management service company. This can provide a reliable and efficient means of running a data centre to agreed cost and performance contractual targets. As it delegates responsibility for such a crucial business resource to an outside supplier, great care must be taken in selecting a supplier and drawing up a contract. Tight management control must be maintained over the performance of the facilities management operation, with agreed corrective actions that can be taken if there are any significant problems.

Automation Data Centre Operations

In the early days of batch mainframes, most operations activities were handled manually, including the loading of programs and data on input devices at the time they were to be run. The scheduling of programs and decisions about which job to run next were largely taken directly by the operator.

The first main element of automation in computer operations was the introduction of operating systems that took over many scheduling and systems control activities. The functioning of an operating system can be tailored to individual installation and applications needs by programs written in special languages, known as *Systems Control Language* (*SCL*) or *Job Control Language* (*JCL*).

A data centre is likely to have many SCL/JCL programs, which can cause difficulties when moving workloads to a different operating system. Expertise in writing SCL/JCL programs is one of the important skills of operations staff. These programs can be extremely complex and powerful, so their production should not be dismissed as a trivial task.

The growing use of online TP networks has added a new dimension and scale to operations requirements. Hundreds of thousands of transactions can be processed by a centre every day, many of which will generate messages for operators or initiate some kind of data centre activity. Workloads have grown in size and complexity to a point where they can no longer be processed on the basis of primarily human operator intervention. A variety of software packages and hardware tools have, therefore, been developed to carry out many data centre functions automatically.

Software is now available to assist in virtually every important data centre function. However, products for specific activities have evolved in a haphazard way from different suppliers, and there are often incompatibilities between them. The foundation of a data centre management strategy should be a plan to integrate all software support within a framework of standard interfaces. A preferred supplier policy may be desirable, although it should allow for some flexibility for products from other suppliers that conform to the standards.

The automation of data centres has led to a steady decline in the demand for operations staff relative to the huge growth in workloads. This trend will continue, but there will always be a need for IS service specialists. At a physical level, operators will continue to carry out manual tasks, like loading tapes, getting disks from a library, putting paper on a printer, sorting out and distributing reports, etc. The numbers of such staff will fall substantially as more activities are automated.

While demand for these relatively unskilled manual jobs will fall, there will be a rise in the importance of highly skilled service personnel who can plan, develop and tune the data centre's capabilities to produce optimum performance. The absolute growth in numbers of these IS professionals may be small compared to the loss of lower skilled operations staff, but they will play an increasingly vital role in the success of the overall IS strategy.

Service Level Agreements

An effective way of maintaining the quality of data centre performance and making IS service management accountable for results is through 'contracts' which define the level of service expected. This places the data centre on the same footing as any other service supplier who makes a contractual agreement with clients.

These *service level agreements* should include precise performance criteria, such as response times, systems availability, success rate in producing printed reports on time and the speed of response to requests for maintenance and emergency help. In return, users must accept responsibility for the costs incurred through their use of the centre's facilities and for providing accurate information on future workload requirements.

Negotiating these agreements can offer a valuable framework for establishing a service management strategy which is of benefit to users and IS service professionals. They give users the chance to help set performance targets that will satisfy their needs. As a result, IS service management will have to provide tangible evidence of what actual performance has been obtained, so that corrective actions can be taken where necessary. For IS service management, they give an agreed basis on which planning can be built with a reasonable degree of confidence. By making users more aware of the costs to the organisation of the services they want, corporate efficiency will also be assisted.

Charging Users for the Service

Traditionally, computers were costed as a corporate overhead, which has two main disadvantages. It reinforces the view that computing is not an integral part of all business activities; and it removes responsibility from users for the IS resources they consume. The overheads method of costing frequently leads to the wasteful usage of storage, processing power, printer paper, etc, because users do what they want, without being made accountable for their applications' impacts on the system as a whole. This makes it difficult for IS service management to balance the requirements of different users and impose appropriate priorities. To do this effectively, in-depth knowledge is needed about the relative corporate value of different applications, as well as having the organisational clout to impose the desired balance.

A *chargeback* system can overcome these problems by getting users to pay for the IS facilities they use. This helps to instil disciplines on users that confine their demands on the service to the ones with the most tangible business benefits. Chargeback can also facilitate the partnership between users and IS management recommended in this book by giving a practical co-operative foundation for determining the optimum workload mix and most cost-effective IS investments. An executive in the data centre may have the final decision on spending to provide adequate service capacity, but always with the agreement of the users concerned.

Chargeability also encourages users to provide detailed estimates of future applications plans. Data centre management must have a realistic idea of the likely growth in the number of workstations, network usage, transaction activity and other workload parameters if they are expected to provide sufficient capabilities to process them satisfactorily.

Structuring Data Centre Responsibilities

The data centre strategy should identify the key activities that must be carried out successfully in order to fulfil service level agreements:

— *operations management* to provide the ongoing service, including *online sessions management* for networked interactive applications;

— *data management* of storage media and the protection of information held on them;

— *performance management* of all hardware, software and telecommunications capabilities;

— *capacity management* to forecast the resources needed to deliver the required service levels;

— *problem management* to co-ordinate the solution of errors and failures;

— *change management* for disciplined control of alterations and enhancements to the system;

— *inventory management* of all installed hardware and software;

— *accounting control* to enable charges to be made for resources used;

— *security control* over the physical environment.

Responsibilities within the data centre must be organised to ensure the necessary attention, resources and control are provided for each activity. The way this is structured will vary considerably between different organisational, data centre and applications circumstances.

Generally, data centre activities can be grouped into five broad categories: *production* (operations and data management); *performance and capacity management; maintenance* (problem management and change control); *administration* (inventory and accounting co-ordination); and *security*. These are discussed in more detail in the following sections.

Providing the Production Service

Operations management is concerned with the day-to-day running of an installation. It involves tasks such as scheduling workloads, dealing with service interruptions, processing and tracking reports, distributing printed output, handling disks and tapes, providing paper to the printer, etc. In some organisations, there may also be a need for *data preparation* services, which could come under the control of the data centre production responsibility. During the period when the vast majority of users provided information for the computer on paper forms etc, many intermediary data preparation staff were needed to key that information into computer storage. The demand for data preparation facilities has fallen substantially since users have been able to input information directly from terminals and workstations.

The management of live online sessions poses many special operational problems. The multitude of messages generated during them must be responded to quickly, such as mounting the tapes containing the files requested. Any service interruption will have a direct impact on users, whereas disruptions to batch processing can often be overcome after some delay, without user results being significantly affected.

With some systems, there are incompatibilities between the methods used to access different applications and systems software. In these cases, it may be possible to achieve concurrent access to many applications only by having different workstations dedicated to particular tasks, or by forcing users to carry out cumbersome procedures when switching between programs, such as logging-off from one application and then logging on to another. Online session management must also aim to provide consistent interfaces to users during their interactive dialogues with different applications. This can be carried out by software which intercepts messages between users and programs, so they can be tailored as necessary.

Data management in a service context is concerned mainly with the use of data storage, rather than the design of data models and DBMS capabilities, which are development functions. Key service data management activities include minimising disk and tape storage requirements; ensuring data is readily available where and when it is needed; and safeguarding stored data at all times.

All production activities can be assisted by software aids, from automatically running batch workloads, through session and dialogue management, to optimising the use of storage media and protecting data. IS service professionals should be continually on the lookout for new software and for opportunities to tune existing software to improve data centre operations.

Performance and Capacity Management

To be of any value, a service level agreement must set precise performance targets. For instance, it should make statements such as 'the system must be available for effective transaction processing for $x\%$ of the expected time' (where x is usually 95% or over). In order to be able to find out if these goals are achieved, data centre management must be able to measure performance in detail and plan ahead to provide sufficient capacity to meet the requirements.

A combination of hardware and software monitors is likely to be needed to check the performance of all system activities. These include factors such as: processor usage; end user response times; traffic on telecommunications lines and through network switches; counts of inbound and outbound characters and messages transmitted; volumes of storage used; number and timing of reports; pages printed; etc. Performance measurement tools must consume minimal system overheads and be easy to apply effectively.

Monitoring network performance is particularly difficult, as it involves collecting data on the activity of many terminals and many telecommunications lines. Some systems use sampling techniques to calculate this traffic; others probe directly into all terminal and line usage.

Capacity planning uses actual performance data, future applications plans and various forecasting techniques to predict the amount of computing capacity needed to handle workloads. This sizing of a system helps to ensure optimum facilities are provided: not too little, which would cause performance problems; not too much, which would waste money. Systematic planning, backed by effective performance modelling tools, can also slow down and minimise the upgrading of system capabilities. Otherwise, there is a tendency to increase resources in a panic if anything goes wrong.

Performance monitoring and capacity planning are directly related to business needs. Poor response time, for instance, can mean irritation and damage to customers, stressful working conditions for staff and, possibly, loss of business. Smooth interfaces between performance monitoring and capacity management systems will be of great benefit. Together, they are a vital foundation to building a service that satisfies user and business goals.

Maintenance and Change Control

The running of complex technical data centre operations is bound to involve dealing with many problems in different activities, from major system bugs to relatively minor logistical difficulties. A disciplined methodology is essential to ensure that these diverse, but interacting, changes are completed correctly and within a co-ordinated plan of testing and integration.

Problem management includes responding to users quickly when service interruptions and faults occur, say through 'hotline' help desks. Problems must be logged and their correction monitored. Data on problems and their fixes should be shared between data centres and other relevant IS functions. Analyses of these problems should identify significant trends and any important areas of particular concern.

The fixing of a problem may lead directly to a change in the system. Other changes are being made continuously by system developers, users, capacity planners, and from many other sources. These should be controlled to ensure they follow appropriate development procedures.

Disruptions to the production service caused by changes should be minimised.

Change control capabilities include the kind of configuration management facilities discussed in Chapter 10, which keep track of the different versions of programs that may be in existence at the same time, so their development and use can be effectively managed.

Administration and Security Control

Service management must handle the administration of all system resources. This will include many items outside the data centre, including those connected via networks. For example, records must be kept of all existing hardware and software installed: their location, who is responsible for them, etc. With so much portable equipment around like PCs, these records are vital to ensure that all elements are being properly and cost-effectively used.

Inventory records help to avoid the phenomenon known as *shelfware*, where a system is bought, experimented with and then left unused in a cupboard. They also help with security by identifying all equipment that must be protected and accounted for. An important administrative activity is to collect information on resource usage, then charge users for the amounts they have consumed. This accounting system must provide detailed breakdowns of how costs have arisen.

Data centre management is likely to be in charge of the preparation and implementation of many of the physical security precautions discussed in Chapter 11. It also needs to be involved in the administration and monitoring of data access security, although built-in locks and the other controls mentioned in Chapter 10 are generally a development responsibility.

SUPPORTING USERS

The prime goal of all IS service management plans is to deliver an efficient and effective user service. This requires the provision of many support facilities other than the data centre capabilities already discussed.

Information Centres

An important technique which has been used to break down the barriers between IS professionals and users is the creation of information centres. They are co-ordinated by the IS function, but are generally outside the data centre and other specialised IS departments and groups. IS service management is likely to play an influential role in running and supporting many information centre capabilities. Plans and goals for information centres must be integrated within the overall IS strategy. If they are not, information centres can take on a momentum of their own, which may eventually lead them to duplicating other IS services and becoming uneconomical and ineffective.

Information centres were first set up primarily as a means of helping users to apply their PCs effectively and to give IS management control over the spread of PCs within a framework that encourages individual user initiative and enthusiasm. These aims have been expanded to include assisting users to access information on data centre computers, develop applications and gain hands-on experience of a variety of other IS benefits. Popular information centre applications have included spreadsheets, using business graphics systems to produce slides and other presentation material, computer-based modelling, decision support systems and statistical analysis software.

The purpose of information centres should be to help users to understand IS capabilities so that they can take more responsibility for exploiting them successfully, backed by IS support. In practice, however, some information centres have permitted IS specialists to carry on doing too much of the work themselves and failed to educate users sufficiently.

The goals and practices of information centres should be reviewed regularly to assess how well they are meeting user and corporate requirements. This should include examining the continuously changing balance between the services offered from information centres and by other IS units. If necessary, an information centre may be closed down after it has served its purpose, with staff and remaining functions re-allocated as appropriate.

A Service for All Reasons

IS service support must cater for many different types of users, applications, organisational groups, locations and technical systems. The pattern of support which is most effective will evolve as these factors change. Support facilities could include:

— help desks to advise users on how to get the most from their systems;

— hotlines for emergency services;

— documentation tailored to users' perceptions of the live service, which may involve integrating suppliers' documentation to tailored service information;

— *service notices*, which could be built into online information systems as well as being printed, informing users of system changes, bug fixes, tips on exploiting facilities, etc;

— maintenance and engineering assistance for all locations and systems in a network;

— advice and help in preparing the physical environment;

— *plus* other IS service activities covered in this chapter.

The delivery of a reliable, responsive, efficient and friendly IS service is crucial to the overall success of an organisation's information management strategy. Much good work in other phases of the strategy can be undone if the daily operational service is below the standards expected. All aspects of providing the service should, therefore, be carefully planned and monitored.

SUMMARY: KEEPING USERS SATISFIED

This chapter has outlined the approach needed to ensure users' day-to-day operational requirements are met satisfactorily. It has stressed the importance of giving due recognition to the significant contribution to IS effectiveness made by service management and staff.

Key elements of the IS service strategy should include:

— a clear plan for integrating the service function with other IS activities;

— a structure which balances central and decentralised operational facilities, taking into account the economic and control advantages of centralised services;

— service level agreements to be used as the basis of precise 'contractual' commitments, with obligations specified for users and IS functions;

— data centre plans, including disciplined methodologies and integrated support tools and techniques;

— selective use of information centres to help users understand and exploit personal computing facilities;

— a systematic and co-ordinated approach to supporting user needs.

This chapter emphasises key themes that have been developed from Chapter 1:

— the value of realistic strategic planning;

— the need for managers to be sensitive to all relevant organisational, business, human, economic and technical factors;

— the importance of continuously monitoring and evaluating how well plans have been implemented to ensure relevant changes are made to meet evolving requirements;

— the overriding aim of keeping the provision of a high-quality business and user service as the prime information management goal.

Appendix 1

Glossary

An alphabetical list of abbreviations follows this glossary of common information management terms. Further explanations of these words and abbreviations, or ones not included in the glossary, can be obtained in the main text of the book, accessed through the index.

Acoustic coupler A device which uses sound signals to link a digital computer system to an analogue telephone connection (see *Modem).*

Acoustic hood A device placed over a printer to reduce its noise.

Ada A high-level language based on structured software engineering principles; named after computer pioneer Countess Ada Lovelace.

Algorithm A set of rules or defined procedures which perform a particular task; a mathematical formula or program procedure.

Analogue A way of representing numerical values by a continuously changing physical quantity, such as electrical wave-form currents or the hands of a non-digital watch.

Analyst workbench A graphics-based system that helps in carrying out the analysis, design and documentation tasks in the front-end of the software development life cycle.

Applications generator Software which automatically generates program code from requirements specifications and designs.

203

Applications software

Programs that carry out the computer functions needed to perform user application tasks, rather than activities oriented to controlling the system's resources (see *Systems software*).

Architecture

1. The blueprint design which defines how the components within a computer system are interrelated.

2. The design of a network showing how the computing and telecommunications capabilities fit together and information flows through them.

3. The internal structure of a computer, such as the number of bits in a basic word length and the set of instructions available to be programmed.

Artificial Intelligence (AI)

The study of how computing can be applied to carry out intellectual, communication and sensory activities in ways that are characteristic of human beings and other animals.

Assembler

1. A low-level programming language (also called an *assembly* language) similar in structure to machine code but using mnemonic instructions and meaningful symbolic addresses that are easier to work with.

2. Software that translates a low-level language into machine-readable code.

Availability

The percentage of time an information system provides a useful service.

Backup

1. Information copied from a computer system regularly and stored separately from current data so that it can be used to reconstitute data to a recent state if the current information is corrupted or destroyed.

2. A computer installation which could be used to run the workload of a system that is out of action for some reason.

3. Duplicate *standby* systems components, like processors, which can be switched to live operation if the existing unit fails.

Bandwidth

Measurement of the information transmission capacity of a telecommunications link (see *Narrowband*, *Wideband*).

BASIC

Relatively easy to learn and use high-level programming language that has been particularly popular on personal computers.

Batch processing

Applications processed sequentially using batched, not online, input, with allowance made for applications' priorities in scheduling the sequence of processing.

Baud

Measurement of data transmission speed, equivalent to bits per second.

Benchmark

A test to measure the performance of a system for a pre-defined workload.

Binary

A representational system that can be in one of two states; the binary digits 0 and 1 are used to process, store and transmit data in digital information systems.

Bit

A single binary digit that takes the value 0 or 1; abbreviation of *bi*nary digi*t*.

Board

A sheet of plastic on which many chips are interconnected to perform particular computing functions (also called *Printed Circuit Board*).

Bug

An error, say in a computer program.

Bureau

A computer services company that offers access, at commercial rates, to its own computing capabilities, such as processors, storage and software packages.

Bus
The part of a computer system's architecture that defines how information is exchanged internally between systems units and how connections are made to external input, output and storage.

Business analyst
A professional with expertise in business applications *and* the systems analysis and design techniques needed for specifying and developing computer-based information systems.

Byte
A group of 8 bits widely used as the length of a coded *character* in computer systems (some architectures have different character bit-lengths).

C
A structured programming language used for many systems software and applications developments.

Capacity management
The function of analysing the computing resources needed to satisfy a given workload, monitoring actual performance and planning for future workload requirements.

Central Processing Unit (CPU)
The main processing control unit in traditional computer architectures (see *Von Neumann architecture*).

Chip
A piece of material, about the size of a fingernail, that contains many integrated circuits used for computer processors and main memory (see *Silicon*).

Circuit switching
Linking systems and devices in a network by directly connecting transmission circuits via switching centres or exchanges, traditional public telephone network.

COBOL

High-level language widely used for commercial applications.

Compiler

Software which translates a high-level language into machine code (see *Interpreter*).

Configuration

1. The hardware elements that comprise a complete system.

2. All software and hardware elements that comprise the complete version of an information system at a particular phase of its life cycle.

Configuration management

The control of various versions of a system that may be in existence at any one time, say in various development, test and operational phases.

Conformance testing

Tests to ensure a system meets a given standard.

Connectivity

The ability to link systems together flexibly and efficiently (see *Open systems*).

Contract staff

IS professionals employed for a fixed contract period, rather than as a permanent employee.

Cost-benefit analyses

Systematic evaluations of the likely costs and benefits of an investment, used to assist making a decision about whether to proceed with a project, how much to invest, etc, (see *Feasibility studies*).

Critical Path Analysis

A technique used for managing projects involving the co-ordination of many activities and tasks (see *Gantt charts*, *PERT*).

Cursor

Pointer on a VDU screen which indicates the current point of activity.

Cybernetics

The study of control and communication in organisations, machines, people and animals.

Daisywheel

A printer mechanism with character printheads at the end of spokes (or petals) around a central hub, which produces letter-quality output.

Data

Synonymous with *information*, but often used mainly for information stored, processed and transmitted by computer-based systems.

Data centre

A centre containing major corporate computing resources, such as mainframes and large amounts of data storage.

Data flow diagram

A design diagram that shows relationships between an information system's data, processes and relevant external factors.

Data model

The analysis and specification of the theoretical organisation, structure and relationships of data in an information system.

Data preparation

The conversion of data from paper documents into computerised digital form.

Data processing

Computer-based information processing typified by the administrative, accounting and commercial applications of traditional mainframe-based systems.

Database

Computerised information organised and structured to optimise its ability to be shared among many users, applications and locations efficiently and reliably.

Database administrator

An IS job function responsible for coordinating the administration and control of a database management system.

Debug   To search for and eliminate errors, part-
                                  icularly in software.

Decision Support System   An IS application which provides access
                                  to information and modelling aids to help
                                  users make decisions.

Desk Top Publishing (DTP)   The application, from ordinary office
                                  desks, of personal computers and work-
                                  stations to carry out the editing, design
                                  layout and other functions involved in
                                  printing and publishing newsletters,
                                  magazines, newspapers, etc.

Discounted cash flow   A cost-benefit analysis technique that
                                  investigates how long it will take for
                                  benefits received to pay for an
                                  investment, anticipating and making
                                  allowance for falling value of money over
                                  time, due to factors like inflation.

Disk   A disk-shaped data storage medium,
                                  coated with magnetic material which is
                                  used to represent binary digits (see *Floppy
                                  disk*, *Hard disk*).

Diskette   see *Floppy disk*.

Distributed processing   An information system where computer
                                  processing capabilities are in many loc-
                                  ations; also known as *distributed com-
                                  puting* or *distributed data processing*.

Dot matrix   A printer mechanism where characters are
                                  formed as a matrix of tiny dots by small
                                  rods.

Dumb terminal   A terminal which does not incorporate
                                  any of its own computer processing
                                  capability and can operate only when
                                  linked online to a computer.

Editor   Software which enables users to edit information stored in a computer, say in desk top publishing and word processing applications.

Electronic Data Interchange (EDI)
An information system where documents and other information are transmitted electronically between different organisations.

Electronic Funds Transfer
An information system that carries out financial transactions, like payments, by purely electronic means.

Electronic mail
The transmission of messages and other communications by purely electronic means, typically in office automation applications.

Electronic Point of Sale
A computer-based system used to record sales at the place where a retail transaction takes place, such as a supermarket checkout.

Emulation
Making one system behave like another, say in predicting the performance of a new computer system before it has been implemented.

End user
A term often used by IS professionals to refer to the person who uses the final computer-based service or product.

Enterprise model
A model of the structure and interaction of a complete organisation or business.

Entity-relation database
A database technique that manages many objects, like documents and program code, in addition to data items.

Ergonomics
The study of the interaction between people and machines to improve overall efficiency, effectiveness, comfort and safety; can be used synonymously with human factors engineering, but is often associated more with the physical aspects of equipment design.

Ethernet	A form of local area network.
Expert system	An application based on a technique that seeks to follow the reasoning processes of human experts, rather than the machine-oriented logic of other programming methods; a form of Artificial Intelligence.
Facilities management	A service which gives an outside supplier management control over all, or part, of an organisation's computing capabilities or IS function, such as running a data centre.
Facsimile communication	Electronic transmission of the image of a document.
Fax	Abbreviation of facsimile.
Feasibility study	The investigation of conditions under which an investment is justified and the detailed requirements for projects that are given the go-ahead.
Field	The basic structural element in a file (see *Record*).
Fifth generation systems	Computer architectures that apply a range of advanced (by 1980s standards) hardware, software and user interface techniques to make systems more intelligent, cost-effective and easy to use.
File	Information organised into an inter-related set of records.
File management	The data management technique based on having separate files for different functions, rather than a common database that integrates and shares data needed for a variety of functions.
Firmware	Software stored in a fixed form, typically on ROM chips (see *Hardwired*).
Flexible manufacturing	An IS application that enables production

processes to be altered quickly and efficiently by changing software controlling many machine tools and Numerical Control machines.

Floppy disk

Disk storage made of thin flexible material contained in cardboard jacket, and which usually holds less data than a hard disk.

Flowchart

A graphical representation of the structure and logical interactions of a system, such as a program; generally applied to non-structured design diagrams.

Formal organisation

The organisational structures and interactions defined by official rules and procedures (see *Informal organisation*).

FORTRAN

A high-level language used for scientific applications.

Fourth generation language

Programming languages and application development aids designed for users who understand the application, rather than for software specialists.

Front-end processor

A system which removes some of the processing load from a central computer, typically by handling some processing and co-ordination at the interfaces between communications lines and the main computing system.

Gantt charts

A graphical representation of the various sub-tasks that need to be performed to complete a project; used in project management techniques like Critical Path Analysis and PERT.

Garbage In/Garbage Out (GIGO)

A warning that incorrect input to a computer system will produce incorrect output, however good the software processing it.

Graceful degradation

The ability of a computer to continue operating, though at a reduced performance level, despite failures in parts of it.

Graphics workstation

A device which can display complex graphical images with good visual quality; includes a screen with a display that is composed of more light dots than conventional screens (known as a *high-resolution* display).

Hacking

Gaining illegal and unwarranted access to information in computer-based systems, often through network links.

Hard copy

See *Printout*.

Hard disk

A rigid magnetic disk, similar to a music record, held in a sealed container and providing higher storage capacity than floppy disks.

Hardware

The physical equipment in a computer system.

Hardwired

Fixed electronic circuit patterns, as used for firmware (see *Microcode*).

High-level language

A programming language designed to match the information processing needs of an application, using commands and statements that are a restricted form of the natural English-language way of expressing a requirement.

Human-computer interaction

See *User/system interaction*.

Human factors engineering

The study of the interaction between people and machines to improve overall operational efficiency, effectiveness, comfort and safety, particularly in working environments; can be used synonymously with ergonomics, but without the emphasis on hardware aspects often associated with that term.

Icon

A graphic symbol on a workstation or personal computer screen which represents a particular function.

Informal organisation

The actual procedures, groups, cliques, communications grapevines, etc, that evolve in an organisation despite the requirements of the formal organisational rules and procedures.

Informatics

Used synonymously with information technology.

Information centre

A unit, outside other specialist IS functions, geared to helping users solve their own computing needs and gain optimum benefit from systems they use directly, such as personal computers and 4GLs.

Information engineering

An integrated, structured approach to the design and development of information systems, encompassing overall organisational and business environments, as well as detailed applications and technical requirements.

Information management

The co-ordination of all information services in an organisation based on a set of policies and techniques covering information collection, organisation, analysis, processing and communication.

Information manager

The senior executive responsible for information management activities.

Information retrieval

The use of a computer-based system to search and extract information from a database or file management system.

Information system

The techniques and tools, often computer-based, which implement information management policies.

Information Technology (IT)

A variety of techniques and devices used to store, process, manage, transmit and communicate information, which can be integrated in unified computing and telecomunications information systems.

Input

Information translated into digital code for processing and storage by computers; as a verb, it means the act of entering data into a computer system.

Integrated circuit

A circuit composed of many transistors which have been reduced in size and placed together on a single physical element, typically a silicon chip.

Integrated Project Support Environment (IPSE)

A variety of tools and techniques unified within a common framework and user interface to cover the IS development life cycle.

Integrated Services Digital Network (ISDN)

A set of standards for a global telecommunications network integrating voice, data, image and text in digitised form.

Intelligent device

A workstation or other device which incorporates its own computer processor, memory and software.

Interactive

An application where the user is involved in a continuous dialogue with the system.

Interface

The junction between two devices, software modules or other elements of a system.

Interpreter

A program that translates a high-level interactive language, like BASIC, into machine code, statement by statement.

Interrupt

When a processor's control unit switches

from one mode to another, say from performing calculations to handling input and output tasks.

Job Control Language   The language used to tell the operating system how to schedule and organise the processing of a computer's workload.

Key   One or more characters that identify a data item or structure, such as a key field in a record or a key word used for information retrieval applications.

Lap-top computer   A compact, portable personal computer about the size of a briefcase.

Laser printer   A high-speed noiseless method of producing good quality printed output from a computer using a laser beam to form images on light-sensitive material.

Letter-quality printing   Printers that produce output of a high enough quality to be used for producing important business letters.

Line printer   A high speed, but often relatively low-quality device that prints a complete line at a time.

Linear programming   An operations research technique which calculates the optimum solution to a problem where the relationship between variables can be represented as a straight line and the result relates to a single factor, such as maximising profits or minimising costs.

Local   Computing capability close to the actual user (see *Remote*).

Local area network   A means of interlinking computers, workstations, storage and other devices within a relatively small area, such as an office or building.

Logging on/off   The procedures needed to initiate and terminate an online session at a workstation or terminal.

Low-level language   A programming language, such as an assembler, that resembles the format of a computer's machine code, but is easier to use because it is not restricted to the use of only numerals.

Machine code   The numeric instructions understood by a computer processor.

Magnetic storage media   Devices, like disks and tapes, which store information as bits according to the magnetisation of tiny elements in the surface of the medium.

Mainframe   The traditional large-scale computers used for corporate data processing; now generally regarded as a system whose power and capability is greater than a minicomputer, but less than a supercomputer, and which is provided with comprehensive support and software from the supplier.

Main memory   High-speed storage which holds the programs and data needed for immediate processing; linked directly to the processor and sometimes regarded as part of the Central Processing Unit.

Management Information Service/System   1. IS applications, like decision support systems, which assist management and staff to carry out their work.

2. The unit responsible for information systems or information management is sometimes called Management Information Services.

Man-Machine Interaction/Interface   See *User/system interaction.*

Manufacturing Automation Protocol (MAP)

An application of the OSI standard for manufacturing production activities.

Memory

Synonymous with computer storage, usually used in relation to main memory.

Menu

A form of user dialogue where the system's next action is determined by the user's choice of an item on a menu of options.

Microcode

Code used in the *microprogram* that translates machine code instructions into appropriate hardware signals; a micro-coded instruction set can be altered relatively easily, whereas a hardwired implementation is fixed.

Microcomputer

The smallest and cheapest complete computers; often synonymous with personal computer.

Microfiche

Microfilm in the form of a rectangular piece of film, like a card, which can be produced as direct output from a computer.

Microfilm

Film that contains reduced images of a document or other information; needs special readers to be seen (see *Microfiche*).

Microprocessor

A processor on a chip.

Microprogram

See *Microcode*.

Mini

Abbreviation for minicomputer.

Minicomputer

A computer of a size and capability roughly between a personal computer and mainframe, sometimes packaged as part of a complete system, like a small business system or word processor; originally more robust and provided with less support than mainframes, but now usually similar to mainframes in many respects (see *Superminis*).

Modelling

The representation of a system's structure and behaviour using mathematical equations, design diagrams and software; can be used to predict likely outcome of various courses of action.

Modems

Devices that translate between the digital code of computers and analogue transmission lines, with one needed at each end of the line; abbreviation for MOdulator-DEModulator.

Module

A self-contained hardware or software unit which interfaces with other modules to form a complete system.

Mouse

A device which moves the cursor on a screen in the same direction as the device is moved.

Multiprogramming

The ability of a computer system to run more than one program at a time.

Multi-tasking

The ability of an operating system to handle more than one user task at a time.

Multi-user system

A computer that allows many online users to share the system's resources and data.

Narrowband

Telecommunications bandwidth that permits a limited volume of information to flow through it, less than a wideband link.

Network

1. The interlinking of many computers, workstations, storage devices, printers and other systems via telecommunications links, according to a structured architecture and defined protocols (see *local* and *wide area networks*).

2. A form of diagram structure used, for example, in project management and database systems.

Node

A focal point in a network or diagram, such as a switching centre or the point on a diagram where lines meet.

Non-procedural language

A programming language which matches the natural way of expressing applications requirements, rather than being oriented towards the algorithmic procedures of languages like BASIC, C and COBOL; fourth generation languages, for example, are often non-procedural.

Number cruncher

Colloquialism for an application that consists primarily of performing many complex calculations.

Numerical control machine

A machine tool controlled by a program on a paper tape loop; computer numerical control machines are based on more sophisticated software methods.

Object-oriented

Programming or design techniques where the basic units are objects that are meaningful to the user in terms of the application, rather than being related to detailed computer structures and requirements.

Online

Activity involving direct interaction with a computer over a communications link.

Open systems

The ability to inter-link computing devices and systems relatively easily and efficiently, based on the implementation of appropriate standards and system architectures; the ISO's Open Systems Interconnection is a key standard for this purpose.

Operating system

Essential systems software which controls

and co-ordinates the scheduling of work processing and use of the system's resources; the prime interface between a computer and applications software.

Operations research

A set of techniques that model systems behaviour using applied mathematics, statistical analysis, probability theory and other disciplines often used in software applications; also known as *operational* research (see *Linear Programming and Modelling*).

Optical Character Recognition (OCR)

An input technique that automatically recognises printed characters, which may need to be in special typefaces.

Optical fibre

High-speed, high-volume telecommunications medium that transmits data as pulses of light down hair-thin glass fibres.

Organisation and Methods

The analysis and design of organisation structures and working methods for office-based activities.

Other Equipment Manufacturer (OEM)

A company which produces a complete system or device including important elements, such as a complete computer, made by another supplier.

Output

The results of computer processing translated into a form that can be understood by users, such as by being displayed on a screen or printed on paper; as a verb, it means the act of delivering results in the desired form.

Packet switching

A method of data transmission where information is sent in a 'packet' that includes an address at the front which is used to route the data to its destination via switching exchanges; alternative to circuit switching.

Page printer

Printers that produce a page at a time, usually of high quality, such as laser printers.

Parallel processing

A computer architecture, such as an *array processor*, which allows many processors to work on the same problem simultaneously.

Parameter

A variable in a program or procedure which needs to have a specific value before the program can run; parameter-driven packages provide a convenient method of tailoring software to specific user needs quickly.

Pascal

A structured high-level language for general software developments; named after French philosopher Blaise Pascal.

Password

A word or number, specific to an individual and/or device, provided during logging-in procedures and used by the system to check authorisation levels when attempts are made to access data.

Payback period

The length of time it will take for the benefits of a system to pay for the investment in it (see *Discounted cash flow*).

Peripherals

Input, output and storage devices in a computer system.

Personal computer

A complete computer that can be used from an ordinary office desk (see also *Lap-top* and *Portable computers*).

PERT

A technique used for managing projects involving the co-ordination of many activities and tasks (see *Critical Path Analysis, Gantt charts*).

Pilot project

An application used to try out a new

system and to learn lessons that make the main live application more successful.

Plotter — Device used for producing graphs and similar drawn output.

Plug-compatible manufacturer — A supplier that makes processors, peripherals, workstations and other equipment which behave in the same way as similar equipment from another manufacturer when connected through a pre-defined interface.

Point of Sale — The place where payment is made for goods in a retail store (see *Electronic Point of Sale*).

Port — Connection points between the internal architecture of a computer and external devices and communications links.

Portability (software) — The ability to move programs between hardware systems with minimal, if any, code changes.

Portable computer — A personal computer compact and light enough to be moved relatively easily; heavier portables are known as *luggables* (see *Lap-top computer*).

Printed Circuit Board — see *Board*.

Printer — Device which produces output on paper; *impact* printers create images by the physical contact of printheads on paper (see *Daisywheel* and *Dot matrix*) and *non-impact* devices without such physical contact (see *Laser printer*).

Printout — Output from a printer.

Private (Automatic) Branch — The switching exchange used within an organisation to link its internal communications system with an external telecommunications carrier; manual systems are non-automatic, but PBX is sometimes also taken to refer to computer-based exchanges.

Procedure

Part of a program that performs a specific task or calculation; an algorithm or *subroutine.*

Process control

Application of a computer to monitor and automatically control, in real time, a continuous production process, such as in the chemical industry.

Processor

The computer hardware unit that performs arithmetic and logic operations, controls the sequence of a system's actions and co-ordinates input, output and storage activities (see *Central Processing Unit* and *Parallel processing*).

Program

A sequence of detailed instructions stored in main memory which automatically controls a computer's actions.

Programming language

A vocabulary and set of rules used to write program code (see *High-level* and *Low-level languages*).

Protocols

A defined set of rules, conventions and other standards that are needed to enable networked information systems to operate effectively.

Punched card/tape

The earliest forms of input, output and storage media, which represent data according to the position of holes punched in a card or paper tape.

Quality management

A set of management techniques and disciplines designed to give assurance that the overall organisational and working environment will produce products and services of optimum quality.

Query-by-example/forms   A means of retrieving information by specifying the items being searched for in the appropriate position of a standard format displayed on a workstation screen.

Query language   An easy-to-learn language used to prepare programs that retrieve information from a database, such as SQL.

Random Access Memory (RAM)   Main memory on a chip which allows users to read from and write to it; read/write memory is a more apt description.

Read Only Memory (ROM)   Main memory on a chip which users can only read from, say because it has a hardwired program.

Real time   The current moment; application where the computer must be able to analyse and respond to inputs instantaneously, as in military defence systems or process control tasks.

Record   A data structure which forms part of a file; usually composed of a number of fields.

Reduced Instruction Set Computer (RISC)   A computer architecture with relatively few basic instructions, which can provide better performance than systems with a larger instruction set.

Relational database   A database management technique that allows great flexibility in establishing relationships between data items, which are stored in two-dimensional tables.

Remote   Computing capability at a distance from the main computing centre or a particular user (see *Local*).

Report generator   Software that allows users to create and change output formats easily, say for display on a screen or a printed report.

Response time

The time taken for the computer to respond to a user input.

Reverse engineering (re-engineering)

The development of well structured and documented software on the basis of existing unstructured and poorly documented code.

Robot

A computer-controlled machine which carries out some, generally limited, human-like movements; typically used on a production line to perform repetitive actions involving restricted 'arm' and 'hand' manipulations.

Scientific management

A management approach which seeks to improve the performance of the organisation as a whole, and each employee within it, by the systematic analysis and planning of working environments to optimise efficiency, based primarily on quantified scientific methods, measurements and control (see *Taylorism*, *Work Study*).

Semiconductor

A substance, such as silicon, that allows the flow of an electronic current to be finely controlled, which makes it suited to the construction of transistors.

Silicon

A semiconductor material, derived from sand, which is the most commonly used substance for making computer chips.

Simulation

The representation of the behaviour of one system by another, often using mathematical and software modelling techniques; *emulation* is a form of simulation that makes one system actually behave like another, rather than using theoretical simulation techniques to show how it is likely to behave.

Sizing	Precise estimation of the processing power, storage capacity and other computing capabilities needed to carry out a predicted application workload to acceptable performance levels (see *Capacity management*).
Socio-technical management	A management approach that aims to optimise overall effectiveness by giving explicit priority to organisational, social and psychological factors, as well as the technological and economic ones emphasised by scientific management techniques.
Software	Generic term for computer programs which control the operation of hardware.
Software engineering	Methodologies, techniques and tools which aim to make software development a more structured, systematic, reliable and predictable process; many computer-aided software (CASE) tools are available to assist with various development activities.
Source code	Software in the language written by the user, before it has been translated into the *object* code, based on machine instructions, needed for computer processing.
Store and forward	An electronic mail capability which stores received information until the recipient requests to see it; sometimes known as an *electronic mailbox*.
Structured Query Language	A widely used query language for relational database management systems.
Structured techniques	Systematic approaches to systems analysis, design and programming which emphasise the importance of building structures from discrete modules in a

disciplined framework, with full documentation; uses structured graphical design diagrams to describe requirements.

Supercomputer

systems with the most powerful processors, used primarily for scientifically-oriented applications involving many complex calculations.

Supermini

Systems at the more powerful end of some minicomputer ranges, overlapping with mainframe capabilities.

Systems analyst

An IS job function responsible for analysing information management requirements and preparing detailed specifications used for selecting and developing appropriate solutions.

Systems engineering

A structured and disciplined approach to the development of a complete hardware and software system, using similar approaches to software engineering.

Systems house

IS services company which sells total hardware and software packages, usually incorporating elements from other suppliers.

Systems integrator

IS services company which takes prime contractual responsibility for supplying a complete information system, made up from products and services from a number of suppliers.

Systems software

Software, such as an operating system, concerned primarily with controlling and co-ordinating computing resources (see *Applications software*).

Taylorism

A common way of referring to scientific management, which was pioneered by F W Taylor.

Technical and Office Protocol

An application of the OSI standard to office activities.

Technology agreement

A negotiated agreement between trade unions and management specifying the conditions under which new computer-based information systems will be introducing, eg including special one-off payments, redundancy arrangements, rest periods for some kinds of stressful work, ergonomic workstation designs to promote operational health and safety, etc.

Teletex

An international standard for electronic mail services which can link to traditional telex networks.

Teletext

A form of videotex which disseminates information by broadcast transmission, say from a television company to TV sets with appropriate built-in teletext converters.

Terminal

A device used for input, output and communications with a computer over telecommunications link; can be synonymous with *workstation*, but generally of more limited and specialised capabilities than workstations.

Time-sharing

A system which handles many online terminals simultaneously.

Top-down design

A structured design approach that starts with the highest level of general concepts or objectives and subdivides them systematically into greater levels of detail.

Transaction processing

Processing discrete user transactions made via online systems, for example making seat reservations.

Transistor

Small electronic device which acts as a switch or amplifier and can be built into integrated circuits for use as computer processors and memory.

Tuple

A record in a relational database.

Turnkey system

A complete computer-based system delivered in a full, finalised form, ready for live operation as soon as it is switched on.

User/system interaction

The aspects of human factors engineering and ergonomics concerned with the techniques of communication between the user and a computer-based information system; synonymous with Human-Computer Interaction and Man-Machine Interaction/Interfaces.

Utilities

Systems software that performs general 'housekeeping' tasks, like optimising the use of storage space.

Value-added network

A networked service which provides IS applications, like electronic mail, in addition to basic telecommunications transmission and switching capabilities.

Value-added reseller

A company which adds facilities and services to a system obtained directly from a supplier before reselling it to users.

Value chain

A method of analysing activities within an organisation to show how value is added at different stages, and in different activities and functions.

Very Large Scale Integration

A measure of the density of integrated circuits on a chip; much greater than *Small*, *Medium* or *Large Scale Integration*, which are chips with the relative degree of integration density described.

Videotex

Computer-based transmission and presentation of information which includes graphics and text, such as viewdata and teletext.

Viewdata   A form of videotex which allows users to interact with databases to retrieve information or carry out transactions.

Visual Display Terminal   Same as a Visual Display Unit.

Visual Display Unit   A device with a display screen and associated keyboard.

Voice recognition   Input technique that interprets human speech directly.

Von Neumann architecture   An architecture built around the concept of a sequential central processing unit; named after computing pioneer John von Neumann.

Wide area network   A network covering a wide geographical area.

Wideband   A telecommunications channel with a high bandwidth that allows larger flows of information, organised in more channels, than narrowband links; also known as *broadband*.

Window   A frame inside an overall workstation screen display within which user tasks can be carried out or information displayed; multi-window systems allow many activities to take place using one screen.

Word processing   Application of computing to the typing process, allowing for greater flexibility in editing text.

Work Study   The analysis and design of organisation structures and working methods in manufacturing operations; an evolution of Taylorism that strongly influenced O&M.

Workstation	A computer system or device that helps people to carry out their jobs; usually has its own intelligence so it can operate on its own or linked into networks with other systems; its capabilities overlap with personal computers, intelligent terminals and VDUs.
X.	A series of communications protocols agreed by the international CCITT telecommunications body and often incorporated into OSI standards, such as X.21 for circuit switching, X.25 for packet switching and X.400 for electronic mail.

ABBREVIATIONS

3GL	Third Generation language.
4GL	Fourth Generation language.
AI	Artificial Intelligence.
ANSI	American National Standards Institute.
ASCII	American Standard Code for Information Interchange.
BASIC	Beginner's All-purpose Symbolic Instruction Code.
bps	bits per second.
CAD	Computer Aided Design.
CAI	Computer Aided Instruction.
CAL	Computer Aided Learning.
CAM	Computer Aided Manufacturing.
CASE	Computer Aided Software Engineering.
CAT	Computer Aided Training or, for medical body scanning systems, Computer Aided Tomography.
CBA	Cost Benefit Analysis.
CCITT	Consultative Committee on International Telephones and Telegraphs (which has representatives from national telecommunications authorities around the world).

CIO	Chief Information Officer.
CNC	Computer Numerical Control.
COBOL	COmmon Business Oriented Language.
CPA	Critical Path Analysis.
cps	characters per second.
CPU	Central Processing Unit.
CRT	Cathode Ray Tube.
DBMS	DataBase Management System.
DCF	Discounted Cash Flow.
DOS	Disk(-based) Operating System.
DP	Data Processing.
DPM	Data Processing Manager.
DSS	Decision Support System.
DTP	Desk Top Publishing.
EDI	Electronic Data Interchange.
EDP	Electronic Data Processing (equivalent to DP).
EFTS	Electronic Funds Transfer System.
EPOS	Electronic Point of Sale.
ER	Entity Relation.
FEP	Front End Processor.
FM	Facilities Management.
FORTRAN	FORmula TRANslation.
G	Giga — one thousand million (usually called 1 billion).
GIGO	Garbage In/Garbage Out.
HCI	Human Computer Interaction.
IM	Information Manager or Information Management.
I/O	Input/Output.

IP   Information Processing.

IS   Information System or Information Service.

ISDN   Integrated Services Digital Network.

ISM   Information System Manager.

ISO   International Standards Organisation.

IT   Information Technology.

JCL   Job Control Language.

K   Kilo — 1000 in decimal; 1024 (2^{10}) in the binary calculations used in computing.

LAN   Local Area Network.

LSI   Large Scale Integration.

M   Mega — 1 million in decimal; 1,048,576 (2^{20}) in the binary calculations used in computing.

MAP   Manufacturing Automation Protocol.

mips   millions of instructions per second.

MIS   Management Information System (or Service).

MMI   Man Machine Interaction (or Interface).

mops   millions of operations per second.

MSI   Medium Scale Integration.

MTBF   Mean Time Between Failures.

NC (or N/C) Numerical Control machine.

O&M   Organisation and Methods.

OCR   Optical Character Recognition.

OEM   Other (or Original) Equipment Manufacturer.

OOD   Object Oriented Design.

OOP   Object Oriented Programming.

OR   Operations (or Operational) Research.

OSI   Open System Interconnection.

PABX	Private Automatic Branch eXchange.
PBX	Private Branch eXchange.
PCM	Plug-Compatible Manufacturer.
PERT	Program Evaluation and Review Technique.
POS (or PoS)	Point of Sale.
PROM	Programmable Read Only Memory.
PSTN	Public Switched Telephone Network (telecommunications network available to the public).
PTT	Post Telephone and Telegraph (describes a national telecommunication authority).
QBE	Query By Example.
QBF	Query By Forms.
RAM	Random Access Memory.
RDBMS	Relational DataBase Management System.
RISC	Reduced Instruction Set Computer.
ROM	Read Only Memory.
SCL	System Control Language.
SQL	Structured Query Language.
SSI	Small Scale Integration.
TOP	Technical and Office Protocol.
TP	Transaction Processing.
VANS	Value Added Network Service.
VAR	Value Added Reseller.
VDT	Visual Display Terminal.
VDU	Visual Display Unit.
VLSI	Very Large Scale Integration.
WAN	Wide Area Network.
WIMP	Window, Icon, Menu, Pointer.
WP	Word Processing.
WYSIWYG	What You See Is What You Get.

Appendix 2

Bibliography

This bibliography provides references to further readings on topics discussed in the book, grouped by subject matter. A brief description is provided if the content is not self-evident from the title of a particular item.

GENERAL MANAGEMENT

Classics and Background Reading

The following are some key 'classics' and other material which cover the history and trends in management studies highlighted in Chapter 3.

Argyris C, Schon D A, *Organizational Learning: A Theory of Action Perspective*, Addison-Wesley, 1978

Babbage C, *The Exposition of 1851*, Frank Cass & Co Ltd, 1968

Barnard C I, *The Functions of the Executive*, Harvard University Press, 1968

Blanchard K, Johnson S, *The One Minute Manager*, Fontana, 1984

Business Fads: What's in and out, *Business Week*, 20 January 1988, pp 40-47

Chandler A D, *Strategy and Structure*, MIT Press, 1978

Crozier M, Implications for the organization, Otway H J and Peltu M, eds, *New Office Technology: Human and Organizational Aspects*, Frances Pinter, 1983

Drucker P F, *Management*, Fontana, 1977

Drucker P F, The coming of the new organization, *Harvard Business Review*, January-February 1988, pp 45-53

George C S, *History of Management Thought*, Prentice-Hall, 1968

Handy C B, *Understanding Organizations*, Penguin, 1985

Harvey-Jones J, *Making It Happen: Reflections on Leadership*, Collins, 1988

Herzberg F, One more time: how do you motivate employees?, *Harvard Business Review*, September-October 1987, pp 109-120

Iacocca L, Novak W, *Iacocca: An Autobiography*, Bantam Books, 1986

Leavitt H J, *Managerial Psychology*, University of Chicago Press, 1985

Likert R, *New Patterns of Management*, McGraw-Hill, 1961

McGregor D, *The Human Side of Enterprise*, Penguin, 1987

Mintzberg H, *The Structure of Organizations*, Prentice-Hall, 1979

Mumford E, *Using Computers for Business Success: The ETHICS Method*, Manchester Business School, 1986

Naisbitt J, *Megatrends*, Futura, 1984

Ouchi, W G, *Theory Z Corporations: How American Business Benefits from Japanese Models*, Addison-Wesley, 1981

Peters T J, Waterman R H, *In Search of Excellence: Lessons from America's Best Run Companies*, Harper & Row, 1982

Pinchot G, *Intrapreneuring: Why You Don't Have to Leave the Corporation to Become an Entrepreneur*, Harper & Row, 1986

Porter M E, *Competitive Advantage: Creating and Sustaining Superior Performance*, The Free Press, 1985

Porter M E, From competitive advantage to corporate strategy, *Harvard Business Review*, May-June 1987, pp 43-59

Porter M E, How competitive forces shape strategy, *Harvard Business Review,* March-April 1979, pp 137-145

Pugh D S, ed, *Organization Theory*, Penguin, 1987 (readings from key writers on organisation structures, management, decision-making and organisational behaviour, including Crozier, Fayol, Herzberg, Likert, Mayo, McGregor, Taylor, Trist, Weber)

Pugh D S, Hickson D J, Hinings C R, *Writers on Organizations*, Penguin, 1988 (describes contributions of prominent figures in the history of management and organisational studies, including many discussed in Chapter 3)

Smith S, Taylorism rules OK? Bolshevism, Taylorism and the technical intelligentsia in the Soviet Union, *Radical Science Journal*, No 13, 1983, pp 3-27

Stewart R, *The Reality of Organizations: Guide for Managers*, Macmillan, 1986

Taylor F W, *Principles of Scientific Management*, W W Norton, 1980

Weber M, *Basic Concepts in Sociology*, Greenwood Press, 1962

Specific Management Techniques

Arnold J, Hope T, *Accounting for Management Decisions*, Prentice-Hall, 1983

Caplen R H, *A Practical Approach to Quality Control*, Hutchinson, 1988

Cohen S S, *Operational Research*, Edward Arnold, 1988

Gray D H, Uses and misuses of strategic planning, *Harvard Business Review*, January-February 1986, pp 89-97

INFORMATION MANAGEMENT STRATEGIES

Impact on Corporate Strategies

A new era for management, *Business Week*, 25 April 1983, pp 34-58 (impact of IT on middle-management organisational structures)

Amdahl Executive Institute, *Business Success and Information Technology: Strategies for the 1990s*, Amdahl Europe, Hartley Wintney, 1988

Leonard-Barton D, Kraus W A, Implementing new technology, *Harvard Business Review*, November-December 1985, pp 102-110

Marsh P, US managers crack the electronic whip, *Financial Times*, 1 October 1987, p 13

Mill J, Room at the top, *Computing*, 5 January 1989, pp 8-9

Otway H J, Peltu M, eds, *New Office Technology: Human and Organizational Aspects*, Frances Pinter, 1983

Otway H J, Peltu M, eds, *The Managerial Challenge of New Office Technology*, Butterworths, 1984

Pounder C, Shaping up to IT, *Computing*, (Magazine Section), 27 February 1986, pp 8-9

Rockart J F, Chief executives define their own information requirements, *Harvard Business Review*, March-April 1979, pp 81-93

Zuboff S, *In the Age of the Smart Machine: The Future of Work and Power*, Basic Books, 1988

Focus on Competitive Advantage

Cash J I, Konsynski B R, IS redraws competitive boundaries, *Harvard Business Review*, March-April 1985, pp 134-142

Miron M, Cecil J, Bradicich K, Hall G, The myths and realities of competitive advantage, *Datamation*, 1 October 1988, pp 71-82

Porter M E, Millar V E, How information gives you competitive advantage, *Harvard Business Review*, July-August 1985, pp 149-160

IS MANAGEMENT

Strategy and Planning

Amdahl Executive Institute, *Clues to Success: IT Strategies for Tomorrow*, Amdahl Europe, Hartley Wintney, 1988

Carlyle R E, Leading IS shops shifting to a centralised structure, *Datamation*, 15 November 1987, pp 17-19

Carlyle R E, Managing IS at multinationals, *Datamation*, 1 March 1988, pp 54-66

Eastlake J J, *A Structured Approach to Computer Strategy*, Ellis Horwood, Chichester, 1987

Hunt G, Corporate commitment and quality management, *Software Management* (as a supplement to *.EXE*), June 1988, pp 18-20

Keen P G W, Planning for successful innovation, Otway H J, Peltu M, eds, *The Managerial Challenge of New Office Technology*, Butterworths, 1984

Nolan R L, Managing the crisis in data processing, *Harvard Business Review*, March-April 1979, pp 115-126

Price Waterhouse, *Managing Information Technology*, Price Waterhouse International, 1989 (annual international surveys)

Sharpe R, Coffey M, Computer services, *Management Today*, December 1987, pp 107-120

Spackman J, How to avoid the worst, *Computer Weekly*, 21 January 1988, pp 18-19 (IS strategy in large organisations)

Sweet F, Milestone management, *Datamation*, 15 October 1986, pp 107-114

Cost-Benefit Analysis

Hopwood A G, Evaluating the real benefits, Otway H J, Peltu M, eds, *New Office Technology: Human and Organizational Aspects*, Frances Pinter, 1983

Lee R, Getting the measure of IT, *Management Today*, December 1988, pp 130-135

Nairn G, Going for IT, *Infomatics*, July 1988, pp 33-44

Parker M M, Benson R J, Information economics: an introduction, *Datamation*, 1 December 1987, pp 86-96

Peltu M, A new approach brings benefits and justifies the investment, *Computing*, 24 April 1986, pp 38-39

Peltu M, IT investment: what can accountants add?, *Computing* (Magazine Section), 13 March 1986, pp 8-9

Peltu M, Measuring the indefinable, *Computing* (Magazine Section), 16 January 1986, pp 8-9

IS Personnel Management

Couger J D, Motivating IS personnel, *Datamation*, 15 September 1988, pp 59-64

Freedland M, What you should know about programmers, *Datamation*, 15 March 1987, pp 91-102

Hartog C, Rouse R A, A blueprint for the new IS professional, *Datamation*, 15 October 1987, pp 65-69

Stamps D, The tough search for telecom talent, *Datamation*, 1 December 1987, pp 65-72

Withington F G, Managing your IS pros, *Datamation*, 15 October 1987, pp 72-81

Implementation and Transition

Butterworth G, Checking off the crowning details, *Computer Weekly*, 3 November 1988, pp 32-33

Duffy F, the office is the computer, *Management Today*, May 1988, pp 93-104

Morgan R, Stedman G, *Computer Contracts*, Oyez Longman, 1984

Ring T, Ways to pay, *Which Computer?*, May 1988

IS DEVELOPMENT

Software Management

De Marco T, *Controlling Software Projects*, Prentice-Hall, 1982

Hall R P, Seven ways to cut software maintenance costs, *Datamation*, 15 July 1987, pp 81-84

Hugo I, When the industry woke up to a crisis, *Computing*, 14 April 1988, pp 24-25 (discussion of first software engineering conference in 1968)

Kalinsky D, Stark facts of software management, *Software Management* (as a supplement to *.EXE*), June 1988, pp 22-24

Mumford E, Successful systems design, Otway H J, Peltu M, eds, *New Office Technology: Human and Organizational Aspects*, Frances Pinter, 1983

Neale A, Tracking software, *Computer Systems*, September 1987, pp 33-35

Rathbone M, Software quality systems, *Computing Techniques*, February 1988, pp 19-34

Remenyi D, Projects from top to bottom, *Computer Weekly*, 8 September 1988, p 38

Symes J, Total control, *Systems International*, August 1988, pp 25-30 (quality management)

The software trap: automate — or else, *Business Week*, 9 May 1988, pp 66-71

Software Engineering

Boehm B W, *Software Engineering Economics*, Prentice-Hall, 1981

Broddle M, Rock-Evans R, Which bench is the best, *Computer Weekly*, 26 January 1986, p 18

Eisner H, *Computer Aided Software Engineering*, Prentice-Hall, 1988

Ince D, Get it right first on the drawing board, *Systems International*, February 1988, pp 55-58, (prototyping)

Jones R, Enter the lexicon, *Datalink*, 19 September 1988, p 15 (data dictionaries)

Jones R, Method actors, *Computing*, 31 March 1988, pp 14-15 (design methodologies)

Jones R, Pack up your troubles in a CASE environment, *Computing*, 27 November 1988, pp 28-29

Jones R, Reversing into the future, *Datalink*, 10 October 1988, pp 14-15 (reverse engineering)

Morgan D, The imminent IPSE, *Datamation*, 1 April 1987, pp 60-64

Page-Jones M, *Practical Guide to Structured Systems Design*, Prentice-Hall, 1988

Simms N, IBM data dictionary gives boost to CASE, *Computer Weekly*, 10 November 1988, p 1

Taylor R, Designer tools for the analyst (plus CASE survey), *Systems International*, May 1988, pp 93-96

Database Management Systems

Anwyll J, Putting a lock on data integrity, *Computer Weekly*, 26 November 1987, p 30

Appleton D S, Rule-based data resource management, *Datamation*, 1 May 1986, pp 86-99

Cramer R A, Things you should know about database systems *Unix/World*, February 1983, pp 28-44

Date C J, *Database: A Primer*, Addison-Wesley, 1986

Hares J, Chipping away at stone tablets, *Computer News*, 19 May 1988, pp 12-14 (relational databases)

Hessinger P R, DBMS: adding value to vanilla, *Datamation*, 1 March 1987, pp 50-54

Jones R, A commanding role, *PC Business World*, 9 June 1987, pp 17-18 (about SQL)

Powell M, Challenging the word of Codd, *Computer Weekly*, 17 March 1988, pp 28-29

Programming

Ince D, Defining the object, *Infomatics*, July 1988, pp 66-71

Jackson M, *Principles of Program Design*, Academic Press, 1975

Meek B, Heath P, *Guide to Good Programming Practice*, Ellis Horwood, 1980

Metzger P W, *Managing a Programming Project*, Prentice-Hall, 1981

Norton M, 4GL survey, *Infomatics*, October 1988, pp 98-114

Robbins C, Getting it write, *Datalink*, 9 November 1987, pp 12-13 (documentation)

Schussel G, Developing a 4GL strategy, *Computer Systems*, June 1987, pp 31-33

Weinberg G, *The Psychology of Computer Programming*, Von Nostrand Reinhold, 1978

Human Factors

ACM Computing Surveys, Volume 14 Number 3, 1983 (complete issue on interactive editing and documentation formatting systems)

Fischer G, Human-computer communication and knowledge-based systems, Otway H J, Peltu M, eds, *The Managerial Challenge of New Office Technology,* Butterworths, 1984

Grandjean E, *The Ergonomics of Computerised Offices*, Taylor and Francis, 1986

Peltu M, *Successful Management of Office Automation*, NCC Publications, 1984, Chapter 5

Rennie A, The human face of design, *Systems International*, August 1988, pp 41-42

IS SERVICES AND OPERATIONS

Data Centre Management

Cartwright I, Strategy for the IBM data centres, *IBM Computer Today*, 4 March 1987, p 14

Fleischer M, Patel S, Shaping up your data center, *Datamation*, 15 November 1988, pp 85-99

Jones P, Planning for the future, *Infomatics* May 1988, pp 92-94

Marcus E, Outfitting the computer room, *Datamation*, 15 July 1986, pp 58-62

Sweet P, At full stretch, *Computing*, 8 February 1988, pp 10-11 (capacity planning)

Sweet P, Someone else's problems, *Infomatics*, September 1988, pp 18-24 (facilities management)

Polston M V, Staffing your 24 hour computer center, *Datamation*, 15 July 1987, pp 75-76

Information Centres

Brzezinski R, When it's time to tear down the info center, *Datamation*, 1 November 1987, pp 72-82

Oglesby J N, Seven steps to a successful info center, *Datamation*, 1 March 1987, pp 73-74

Stephenson M, Learning how to say 'no' at the right time, *Computing*, 8 October 1987, pp 32-33

Security and Data Protection

Data Protection Act: Special report, *The Guardian*, 9 November 1987, p 14

Davies D, Anatomy of a disaster, *Computer Law and Security Report*, March-April 1988, pp 35-36

Is your computer secure?, *Business Week*, 1 August 1988, pp 50-56

Lammer P, Protection from infection, *Systems International*, June 1988, pp 75-76 (software viruses)

Rothstein P J, How to ensure disaster recovery, *Datamation*, 15 October 1988, pp 86-89

Shain M, Playing safe, *Communications Management*, October 1988, pp 17-22

IS APPLICATIONS

Ellis W, Reaping benefits 'just in time', *Financial Times*, 2 April 1986, p 18

Garnett N, Man struggling to master the machine, *Financial Times*, 14 October 1988, p 21 (computer integrated manufacturing)

Hirscheim R A, *Office Automation: Concepts, Technologies and Issues*, Addison-Wesley, 1985

Holdsworth I, EFT/POS gets the go-ahead, *Computer Weekly*, 3 September 1987, pp 18-19

Keen P G W, Scott Morton M S, *Decision Support Systems: An Organizational Perspective*, Addison-Wesley, 1978

Large J, How networks net business, *Management Today*, February 1987, pp 86-94 (use of IS networks in many industries)

Manufacturing Automation Protocol: A Special Report, *Industrial Computing*, July 1988, pp 10-28

Martin J, *The Wired Society*, Prentice-Hall, 1978 (general impact of IT)

Owen W, Computers: toy or tool?, *Management Today*, December 1988, pp 114-129 (senior management use of desk top computers)

Peltu M, *The Electronic Office*, BBC Publications, 1984

Richardson A, Trading without paper, *Systems International*, January 1988, pp 19-23 (EDI applications)

Schatz W, EDI: putting the muscle in commerce and industry, *Datamation*, 15 March 1988, pp 56-64

Sharpe R, Coffey M, The automated office, *Management Today*, March 1987, pp 87-110

The portable executive, *Business Week*, 10 October 1988, pp 40-47 (management use of personal computers and other information systems)

Weizenbaum J, *Computer Power and Human Reason*, Penguin, 1984 (critical examination of the extent and limitations of computer-based systems)

Wiggin G, The golden rules of global networking, *Datamation*, 1 October 1987, pp 68-73

IT BACKGROUND

Evans C, *The Making of the Micro*, Gollancz, 1981

Feigenbaum E A, McCorduck P, *The Fifth Generation*, Addison-Wesley, 1983

Payne M, Data communications, *Computing Techniques*, June 1987, pp 52-56

Peltu M, *Introducing Computers*, NCC Publications, 1983

Sheil B, Thinking About Artificial Intelligence, *Harvard Business Review*, July-August 1987, pp 91-97

Simons G L, *Towards Fifth-Generation Computers*, NCC Publications, 1983

The OSI Handbook, ICL, 1987

Underwood S, ISDN on trial, *Datamation*, 1 February 1987, pp 52-56

Wiener N, *Cybernetics: or Control and Communication in the Animal and the Machine*, MIT Press, 1961

Index